An Official Whitman® Guidebook

WHITMAN INSIDER GUIDE
Collecting State Quarters
and Related Coins

Whitman Publishing, LLC
Atlanta, GA

© 2006 Whitman Publishing, LLC
3101 Clairmont Road · Suite C · Atlanta, GA 30329

Certain portions of the narrative of this book are excerpted or condensed, with permission, from *A Guide Book of Washington and State Quarters* (Bowers, 2006).

Correspondence concerning this book may be directed to the publisher, at the address above.

ISBN: 0-7948-2015-8
Printed in China

For a complete catalog of numismatic reference books, supplies, and storage products, visit Whitman Publishing online at

www.whitmanbooks.com

Coin collecting has long been an enjoyable pastime in this country, but the kinds of coins saved, and the way they are acquired, is constantly evolving. It is no longer possible to find obsolete or rare coins in circulation. Gone are the days when a collector could pluck gold or silver coins from pocket change. These changes have made it necessary for the new generation of collectors to find other ways to satisfy their interest.

Throughout the past 40 years collectors have had only a few opportunities to find variety or excitement in their money. Basic coin designs have changed very little in the past 65 years. Newly introduced dollar coins, bullion pieces, and commemorative coins are not in circulation. The coins that are in frequent use do not suffer from excessive wear, and seem commonplace.

With these obstructions in mind, in 1997, a small group of active collectors petitioned the government to consider a radical coinage program that would recognize each of the 50 states, and serve as an educational device for all who used them. A secondary motivation was to stimulate interest in the hobby of coin collecting.

The popularity of the 50 State Quarters® Program is evident everywhere. The new quarters are fun to collect, and have fostered a renewed interest and pride in the history of our great Union. Their story, as told in this book, will add to your enjoyment of collecting them.

Kenneth Bressett
Colorado Springs, Colorado

Kenneth E. Bressett is a numismatic historian and author or editor of more than a dozen related books; a past governor, vice president, and president of the American Numismatic Association; and a highly accomplished teacher, researcher, and student. He has served for many years as the editor of *A Guide Book of United States Coins*, popularly known as the "Red Book." As a former consultant to the United States Mint, he was instrumental in originating the 50 State Quarters® Program and in selecting many of the coins' reverse designs.

1776 Continental Currency

This early American note, issued by the Continental Congress in 1776, names the original 13 colonies: Delaware, Pennsylvania, New Jersey, Georgia, Connecticut, Massachusetts, Maryland, South Carolina, New Hampshire, Virginia, New York, North Carolina, and Rhode Island. They are symbolized as strong, interlocking links in an unbreakable chain. (The same design was also featured on the metal 1776 Continental dollar.) These would be the first 13 states honored in the new quarters program.

THE STATE QUARTER PROGRAM

State quarters: since 1999, these collectible coins have captured the imagination of millions of Americans! Serious collectors, or *numismatists*, fill their collections with one coin from each mint (Denver, Philadelphia, and San Francisco), in shiny Mint State or even in specially struck Proof finish. Some specialists look for state quarters with errors, like the Wisconsin quarter with an extra leaf on its ear of corn. Millions of other people—who might not collect any other coins—eagerly check their pocket change to see what's new… to find a quarter honoring Florida, New York, Texas… to collect their home states, their favorite vacation states, or one from every state in the Union.

Every year during the program the United States Mint issues five new designs, each featuring a different state in the order in which they joined the Union or ratified the Constitution. In the *Whitman Insider Guide to Collecting State Quarters* you will learn all about these remarkable coins—fascinating in their diversity, unequalled in their historical importance, and affordable enough that everyone can collect them.

THE UNITED STATES MINT

As a bit of background: beginning with the new commemorative coin program launched by Mint Director Donna Pope in 1982, the Bureau of the Mint (as it was then called) went into high gear with innovative marketing concepts. Since then, many different and interesting Proof and commemorative coin sets have been offered in various purchase options.

Similarly, since the inception of the state quarters program in 1999 the Mint has shown great creativity, and along the way new ideas have been implemented. Recent offerings include small 100-coin bags of individual issues, as well as 1,000-coin bags, and rolls. From a financial and popularity viewpoint, the entire program has been a spectacular success.

The United States Mint has done much in its outreach to collectors in recent decades. This includes the administrations of Mint directors Philip Diehl, Jay Johnson, and Henrietta Holsman Fore (who left the post in August 2005), as well as Acting Director David A. Lebryk, during the state quarters program from 1999 to date. The Mint's outreach is likely to continue under successive directors. Collectors and numismatic writers have been warmly welcomed, exhibits have been mounted at conventions, and much information has been supplied to numismatic periodicals. There has never been a better time to be a coin collector.

A NEW COIN FOR THE NATION

In 1999, the United States Mint launched the 50 State Quarters® Program. Its premise: each year through 2008, five states would recommend designs for the reverse of the quarter dollar, the motifs depicting a claim to fame, or some aspect of the state's history, traditions, or natural scenery.

Most states called for design suggestions to be submitted by their citizens, to be reviewed by the governor and advisors, after which a single design would be selected. The selected design would be submitted to the Commission of Fine Arts (an advisory group), the Citizens Commemorative Coin Advisory Committee, and the United States Mint, after which certain modifications might be made.

These suggestions would be limited only by the imagination—and the rule that no busts, state seals, state flags, logotypes, or depictions of living people would be included. And of course the artist's work would ultimately be constrained to a 24.3 mm circle (a little less than an inch—the diameter of the quarter dollar).

Each year's five quarters have been released in the order their states ratified the Constitution or joined the Union—roughly one new coin design every 10 weeks. Many have been launched with ceremonies attended by Mint officials and dignitaries. Circulation-strike coins (those struck for day-to-day business) have been made at the main mint in Philadelphia and the branch mint in Denver, while the San Francisco Mint has struck Proof coins for collectors, in copper-nickel composition as well as in silver.

In the January 19, 1999, issue of *Numismatic News*, Mint Director Philip M. Diehl wrote about the start of the program:

> The idea of a circulating commemorative has been around the hobby for decades, but frankly, good ideas are a dime a dozen. Far more rare is the ability to move an idea to reality, especially in the rough and tumble environment of Washington, DC.
>
> From my vantage point, the lion's share of the credit for making the 50 States program a reality goes to David Ganz, for his persistence as an advocate, and Congressman Michael Castle, for championing the proposal through Congress. David gradually persuaded me of the merits of the proposal, and we at the Mint, in turn, convinced Treasury and the Hill it was doable. There are other claimants, to be sure, but the hobby owes a debt of gratitude to Congressman Castle and Mr. Ganz.

OBVERSE CHANGES

To accommodate the creative designs intended for the reverse of the state quarters, the inscriptions UNITED STATES OF AMERICA and QUARTER DOLLAR were relocated to the obverse (the "front" or "face" of the coin), above and below the portrait, respectively. LIBERTY and IN GOD WE TRUST were moved to new positions. At the same time the Mint decided to "improve" the portrait of Washington by adding little curlicue-and-squiggle hair details.

THE PROGRAM TAKES OFF

The first coin in the series, struck for the state of Delaware, shows Caesar Rodney, a famous figure from the state's colonial history. It was produced in 1999. The rest of the first year's coins were struck

A Changing Portrait
George Washington's portrait has appeared on the quarter dollar since 1932. In 1999, for the state quarter program, the Mint added more detail to the president's periwig.

for Pennsylvania, New Jersey, Georgia, and Connecticut. The general public's reception was enthusiastic, and numismatists were pleased as well. For this and other quarters as they were developed, *Coin World* and *Numismatic News* carried week-by-week coverage, beginning with early design ideas and concepts, through sketches, continuing to the approved motifs, coinage, and distribution.

A SOMETIMES BUMPY RIDE

Selecting a single design to truly embody a state has not always been easy. Controversies have erupted—and not only over the motifs chosen. Sometimes an artist would find that the state-approved design was dramatically altered by the Mint staff. In practice, it was the Mint that made most of the final decisions, and not the advisory committees. In particular, there was a controversy with the 2003 Missouri motif, for which the Mint vastly changed the artist's work, although there were other complaints as well. It seemed that neither the artist's original sketch nor the Mint revision were appreciated, and today the Missouri design wouldn't make any "best of the series" list.

What makes a *great* design different from an "also-ran" is subjective—beauty is in the eye of the state quarter beholder. Numismatic writer and historian Q. David Bowers says this about the series' artistry:

> To my eyes, coins that had a main focal point, such as the 1999 Delaware with its horse and rider, the 2001 North Carolina with the Wright biplane and the 2003 Maine with its lighthouse prominent on a rockbound coast, are more artistic than motifs in which a bunch of things are scattered, as with the 2003 Illinois, 2003 Arkansas, and 2004 Florida.

In an October 2002 issue of *Coin World*, columnist Michele Orzano observed:

> Often those state quarter dollars with a single focus seem to "click" with collectors, especially with those who have no

knowledge of the states' histories or achievements. Collectors should be learning something when they see these coins....

It would do well for those states that have yet to select designs to keep in mind the effect a single theme or design element can achieve. Considering the very small "canvas" artists have to work on, avoiding a cluttered look may be the best choice. That observation doesn't mean designs featuring more than one element are bad. However, those selecting designs, as well as those submitting them, may want to keep in mind less is really more.

During the Missouri contretemps, Paul Jackson, designer of the sketch picked for the quarter, mounted a vigorous campaign against the United States Mint. Somewhat overlooked was the fact that the Commission of Fine Arts didn't like the idea of multiple design elements, but preferred a single-theme rather than conflicting motifs.

Perhaps reasonably, perhaps overreacting after being stung by the criticism, the Mint rewrote the rules of the design process, to be effective with the designs of 2005.

NEW MINT RULES OF 2005

Stage 1: The United States Mint will initiate the formal state design process by contacting the state governor approximately 24 months prior to the beginning of the year in which the state will be honored. The governor, or such other state officials or group as the state may designate, will appoint an individual to serve as the state's liaison to the United States Mint for this program.

Stage 2: The state will conduct a concept selection process as determined by the state. The state will provide to the United States Mint at least three, but no more than five, different concepts or themes emblematic of the state; each concept or theme will be in narrative format. The narrative must explain why the concept is emblematic of the state and what the concept represents to the state's citizens. A narrative that merely describes a particular design is not acceptable.

Stage 3: Based on the narratives, the United States Mint will produce original artwork of the concepts, focusing on aesthetic beauty, historical accuracy, appropriateness and coinability. If the state has not provided at least three concepts, the United States Mint may produce additional concepts for the state.

Stage 4: The United States Mint will contact the state to collaborate on the artwork. The state will appoint an historian, or other responsible officials or experts, to participate in this collaboration to ensure historical accuracy and proper state representation of the artwork. The United States Mint will refine the artwork before forwarding it to the advisory bodies.

Stage 5: The Citizens Coinage Advisory Committee and the U.S. Commission of Fine Arts will review the candidate designs and make recommendations and the United States Mint may make changes to address such recommendations.

Stage 6: The United States Mint will present the candidate designs to the Secretary of the Treasury for review and approval.

Stage 7: The United States Mint will return to the state all candidate designs approved by the Secretary of the Treasury.

Stage 8: From among the designs approved by the Secretary, the state will recommend the final design through a process determined by the state, within a time frame specified by the United States Mint.

Stage 9: The United States Mint will present the state's recommended design to the Secretary for final approval.

MORE ON THE COMPLICATIONS

The background to the new rules was described by reporter Don Hamilton (of the *Portland Tribune*) in connection with the design selection for the 2005 Oregon quarter. He quoted two writers on the subject:

> "Designs created little controversy when the first five quarters were issued in 1999," said Michele Orzano, senior staff writer for *Coin World* magazine. But the process grew more complicated as the program gained wider attention. Bigger selection committees. More school kids. Greater public involvement. In some states, the process became unwieldy. "They didn't have any idea how passionate people can become about this," Orzano said. "You're not going to make everybody happy."
>
> And compromise doesn't always produce the most compelling art. "Most of the designs are boring, timid, and cluttered evidence of all that can go wrong when art is created by committee," wrote Carol Vinzant in *Slate*, the online magazine.

Of course, opinions on such matters can vary, and widely. No doubt the average collector would not agree with Ms. Vinzant, that *most* of the designs were truly bad.

This new process effectively ended the idea of tapping the talents of artists, amateur and professional, in the private sector.

ARTISTIC INFUSION

The year 2004 brought a novel new element to the state quarters, when the United States Mint implemented its Artistic Infusion Program. This was an effort to bring the talents of private-sector artists under the wing of the government. Under this program, eighteen "master designers" and six "associate designers" would create motifs for American coins and medals.

Only one of the master designers was credited with having any coin experience, he being Bill Krawczewicz of Severna Park, Maryland, listed as a bank note designer, currently with the Bureau of Engraving and Printing, and a "designer of U.S. commemorative coins and state quarter dollars" (the coins not being specified in the announcement). Q. David Bowers was able to determine that the commemorative coins were certain issues beginning with the 1993 Bill of Rights dollar. Bowers notes that "the 'state quarter *dollars*' required more outside investigation after which one (singular, not plural) design was tracked down, that of the 2000 Maryland coin."

An orientation meeting was held at the Philadelphia Mint in February 2004. "Together, we will invigorate the artistry of coin design in America," Mint Director Henrietta Holsman Fore announced.

Under the Artistic Infusion Program, each master designer receives $1,000 for each sketch submitted, while associates receive $500. In contrast, Daniel Carr, a private-sector artist, was paid $2,500 for each of his earlier sketches used on quarters. Paul Gilkes, in the July 5, 2004, issue of *Coin World*, gave some good news for the artists and engravers (concerning regular coins and medals) and some bad news (for their state quarter artistry):

FROM CONCEPT TO COIN

California state quarter designer Garrett Burke (pictured here with his wife Michelle, a coin collector) started with a question: "What does California mean to me?"

His notes led to rough sketches centering on natural themes, with writer/poet/conservationist John Muir connecting man to Nature.

Burke's final contest entry was finessed at the Mint (a). Their final rendering (b) led to the California state quarter (c), one of the most popular coins in the series.

California governor Arnold Schwarzenneger (shown with design review committee member Dwight Manley, coin collector Penny Marshall, and wife Maria Shriver) praised the "beautiful, beautiful design."

The Artistic Infusion Program artists will also receive other new coin and medal assignments as they become available. The initials of both the artists and the engravers will be on all coins and medals, except the 50 state quarters, which will carry only the sculptor-engravers' initials.

DIVERSITY IN DESIGNS

If anything, the state quarter designs have been diverse. No two have been precisely alike, but some have been similar. North Carolina (2001) and Ohio (2002) both feature a Wright brothers' biplane as the motif. The coins of Kansas (2005) and North Dakota (2006) both show the American bison. And the quarters of Kentucky (2001) and Nevada (2006) are occupied by horses—that of the former fenced in, those of the latter running wild.

Many state quarters have included inscriptions familiar only to the citizens of the state or to trivia experts. Do you know which state is THE CROSSROADS OF AMERICA? Which one has a FOUN-DATION IN EDUCATION, or which is linked to the CORPS OF DISCOVERY, or is considered the CROSSROADS OF THE REVOLUTION? (Answers in order: Indiana, Iowa, Missouri, and New Jersey.)

In 2004 Governor Arnold Schwarzenegger made the final selection for the 2005 California quarter. The design featured John Muir, a famous naturalist. Some observers would have preferred a Gold Rush motif, tied to the state's history. In fact, a Gold Rush design had been submitted, but is was more of an assortment of objects, rather than a strong central motif (as on the dynamic 1925 California Dia-mond Jubilee commemorative). Still, the John Muir design, which also featured a view of a California condor flying over Yosemite National Park, has proven itself a numismatic favorite.

In the process of creating these quarters, many diverse designs have been born—some beautiful, others homely; some logical, others need-

(From *Across the Continent* by S. Bowles, 1853)

ing explanation, again with all of these factors in the eyes of the beholder. As each design has been created by a different artist, and as there have been nearly as many different themes as there have been states observed, the result is a fascinating numismatic panorama. In general, the program has been well appreciated by the coin collector community and has been considered a high point in recent Mint

The Washington quarter wasn't the first piece of Americana to portray "The Father of His Country." In the 1850s, tokens and medals depicting the first president were hot collectibles. That popularity cooled somewhat after the early 1860s, but so-called Washingtonia remained popular into the next century and beyond. The 1932 Washington quarter dollar was first struck to commemorate the 200-year anniversary of his birth. (Painting by Henry Alexander Ogden, published by the U.S. Army Quartermaster General in 1890)

history. Indeed, it has been one of the greatest boons ever to numismatics, encouraging millions of people to pay closer attention to their pocket change.

MORE CHANGES IN THE FUTURE?

From the very start of the program some have suggested that the 50-state concept should be extended to include the District of Columbia and territories and possessions such as Puerto Rico and Guam. This comment by David L. Ganz appeared under the title "Senate Seeks Quarter Extension," in *Numismatic News*, August 3, 2004:

> Hopes that Congress will extend the state quarter program with an 11th year that will include Washington, D.C., and five insular territories took a boost July 8 when Sen. Bill Nelson, D-Fla., introduced S. 2626, a bill to provide for a circulating quarter dollar coin program to honor the District of Columbia, the Commonwealth of Puerto Rico, Guam, American Samoa, the United States Virgin Islands, and the Commonwealth of the Northern Mariana Islands.

Will the fifty state quarters be joined by additional coins in 2009? If so, what will their designs look like? We will all have to stay tuned to watch developments.

KEY TO COLLECTING STATE QUARTERS

In all instances, for both copper-nickel clad and 90% silver state quarters, circulation-strike mintages have run into the hundreds of millions and Proof mintages in the high hundreds of thousands. Accordingly, the four varieties of each issue (Philadelphia, Denver, clad Proof, and silver Proof) were readily available in the year they were minted, and after that time the market supply has been generous.

Collecting state quarters can lead to a deeper exploration of each state's numismatic history. Many of the 13 original colonies struck coins in the 1700s. Some states had commemorative silver half dollars

**Former U.S. Mint Director Henrietta Holsman Fore
at the Wisconsin State Quarter Launch Ceremony**

Most state quarter launches involve schoolchildren, state dignitaries, local enter-
tainment, and Mint officials, as well as the general public. At the launch of the
Wisconsin quarter, Wayne Larrivee, voice of the Green Bay Packers, was master of
ceremonies. The Colby Elementary School Choir sang the "Star Spangled Banner."
Mint engraver Alfred Maletsky received a wheel of Colby cheese—made only in
Wisconsin—just like the one he modeled for the quarter design. For good measure
he was given an ear of corn as well.

minted in their honor in the 1900s. In addition to examining each state quarter, the *Whitman Insider Guide to Collecting State Quarters* offers insight on related coins, tokens, paper money, and other collectibles. You can branch out and build an attractive and historical collection based around your state quarters, adding older and even more exotic pieces for an appealing display.

Coins are enjoyable to contemplate. Perhaps that is the most important key to collecting state quarters: have fun with them! Study their designs as miniature works of art; explore their history; look for symbolic meanings and connect their motifs to the states they represent. Which design is your favorite? Which ones do you *not* like, and why? Probably if 500 collectors were polled, no two lists would be identical. The coins are as unique and diverse as the citizens of our great nation.

And with that thought we begin our exploration of the 50 state quarters...

DELAWARE

The first coin out of the gate, so to speak, was widely appreciated by collectors. It shows Caesar Rodney on horseback, on an 80-mile ride to Philadelphia, then the seat of the Continental Congress. On July 1, 1776, despite severe discomfort and illness, as a delegate from the colony of Delaware he cast the deciding vote that called for independence from

1 of 50

England. History records his many accomplishments, including as a signer of the Declaration of Independence, a soldier, and as the holder of many offices in the state.

Citizens of the state were invited to send ideas for the design to the Delaware Arts Council, resulting in over 300 entries. Certain of these were sent to the Mint, where they were converted into drawings. Three concepts were selected: Caesar Rodney; a symbolic Miss Liberty; and a quill-and-pen design. The office of Governor Thomas R. Carper conducted a poll, and the Rodney concept won almost twice as many votes as the other two combined.

There is no known portrait of Caesar Rodney, so one artist's guess at his appearance is as good as any other's. The Mint faced a similar situation in 1892, for the design of the commemorative half dollar of the World's Columbian Exposition: nobody knows for certain what Christopher Columbus actually looked like. Artistic license was not only allowed, but necessary.

The Blue Hen Chicken and the Peach Blossom, symbols of Delaware

MINTAGE FIGURES

Circulation Coins (copper-nickel)	Proof Coins (copper-nickel)	Proof Coins (silver)
1999-P: 373,400,000 1999-D: 401,424,000	1999-S: 3,713,359	1999-S: 804,565

NUMISMATIC NOTES

Delaware issued many types of currency in its colonial era.

1936 Delaware Tercentenary Half Dollar

This coin commemorated the 300th anniversary of the landing of the Swedes in Delaware. According to the *Guide Book of United States Coins* (popularly known as the "Red Book"): "The colonists landed on the spot that is now Wilmington and established a church, which is the oldest Protestant church still used for worship. Their ship, *Kalmar Nyckel*, is shown on the reverse of the coin, and the Old Swedes Church on the obverse. ... The anniversary was celebrated in 1938 in both Sweden and the United States."

Coin is shown enlarged.

PENNSYLVANIA

The 1999 Pennsylvania quarter features a collage of items relating to the state: an outline map, a representation of the 14' 6" statue (Commonwealth) from the top of the State Capitol building, a keystone, and a motto.

2 of 50

A *keystone* is the top stone in an arch—the final stone placed. Pennsylvania's nickname of "The Keystone State" dates back to a Jefferson Republican victory rally in October 1802, where the state was toasted as "the keystone in the federal union." A U.S. Mint press release for the state quarter further notes the "key position of Pennsylvania in the economic, social, and political development of the United States."

The Pennsylvania quarter was initiated with the first official launch ceremony in the program, on March 9, 1999, at the Philadelphia Mint. The governor, federal officials, and others were there. About two dozen fifth-graders from the General George A. McCall Elementary School were invited guests. Many of those on hand were allowed to push a button to set in motion an 82-ton press to strike the Pennsylvania quarter.

The Ruffed Grouse and the Mountain Laurel, symbols of Pennsylvania

MINTAGE FIGURES

Circulation Coins (copper-nickel)	Proof Coins (copper-nickel)	Proof Coins (silver)
1999-P: 349,000,000 1999-D: 358,332,000	1999-S: 3,713,359	1999-S: 804,565

NUMISMATIC NOTES

Pennsylvania has a long numismatic history. The capital city of Philadelphia was the first seat of the young nation's federal government; it was from here that the Continental Congress issued paper money and pewter Continental dollars. The city would later become a center of banking in the United States, and of course the home of the U.S. Mint.

1936 Battle of Gettysburg Half Dollar

This commemorative coin was struck to memorialize the famous Civil War battle, a watershed in state (and national) history.

A view of the original U.S. Mint buildings at Philadelphia. (Watercolor by Edwin Lamasure Jr.)

NEW JERSEY

The 1999 New Jersey quarter furnished the first truly familiar motif on a state coin: the well-known scene taken from the 1851 painting by Emmanuel Gottlieb Leutze (1816–1868), *Washington Crossing the Delaware*. This scene was also used in 1976 for 13¢ postage honoring the nation's Bicentennial, and in the late 1800s it was part of the design for $50 National

3 of 50

Bank Notes. Accordingly, it may be proper to credit Leutze as the designer of the coin.

The original painting now resides in the Metropolitan Museum of Art in New York City.

Washington Crossing the Delaware

Americans in the late 19th century would marvel at the general's brave excursion on the back of the $50 National Bank Note.

The Eastern Goldfinch and the Violet, symbols of New Jersey

MINTAGE FIGURES

Circulation Coins (copper-nickel)	Proof Coins (copper-nickel)	Proof Coins (silver)
1999-P: 363,200,000 1999-D: 299,028,000	1999-S: 3,713,359	1999-S: 804,565

NUMISMATIC NOTES

In May 1682, the New Jersey legislature made Irish St. Patrick's coinage legal tender in the colony. Later the colony issued many types of currency. In the 1780s, New Jersey coppers were produced under private contract.

**Copper New Jersey
Coin of 1786**

On June 1, 1786, the New Jersey colonial legislature granted to Thomas Goadsby, Albion Cox, and Walter Mould the authority to coin three million copper pieces. These were to be valued at 15 to a shilling. "In any operation of this kind, the contractors purchased the metal and assumed all expenses of coining. The difference between these expenses and the total face value of the coins issued represented the profit." (*A Guide Book of United States Coins*, 2007 edition)

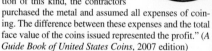

2004 Thomas Edison Silver Dollar

The famous inventor's new laboratory was opened in West Orange, New Jersey, in 1887. Edison was honored on a commemorative silver dollar in 2004.

GEORGIA

The 1999 Georgia quarter features a montage of topics relating to the state, similar in concept to the Pennsylvania issue. An outline map of the state has at the center a peach, the best-known symbol of that southern district. The official state tree, the live oak, is depicted by appropriate branches, one on each side of the coin. On a flowing ribbon is the motto, WISDOM JUSTICE MODERATION.

4 of 50

MINTAGE FIGURES

Circulation Coins (copper-nickel)	Proof Coins (copper-nickel)	Proof Coins (silver)
1999-P: 451,188,000 1999-D: 488,744,000	1999-S: 3,713,359	1999-S: 804,565

James Oglethorpe was the wealthy English soldier and philanthropist who colonized what became the state of Georgia. He secured a charter for the colony in 1732; his idea was to begin a refuge for unemployed debtors freshly released from prison.

**The Brown Thrasher
and the Cherokee Rose,
symbols of Georgia**

Numismatic NOTES

Georgia issued many types of currency during colonial times. In 1830, Templeton Reid, an assayer and coiner, struck $2.50, $10, and $20 coins at Milledgeville, then at Gainesville. The Dahlonega Mint opened in 1838 to make coins from the gold mined in the area; it operated continuously until partway through the Civil War (1861).

1925 Stone Mountain Memorial Half Dollar

Struck on January 21, 1925, the birthday of General Thomas "Stonewall" Jackson, this coin shows Jackson and General Robert E. Lee on horseback. Proceeds supported the carving of the Stone Mountain memorial outside Atlanta, Georgia.

Olympic Commemoratives of 1995

The Olympic Games held in Atlanta in 1996 were the subject of several coins struck in 1995.

Some coins are shown enlarged.

CONNECTICUT

Q. David Bowers states that a numismatist "could make a specialty, or at least a side activity, in assembling a collection of coins, tokens, medals, and paper money featuring the Charter Oak."

5 of 50

The 1935 Connecticut Tercentenary half dollar features the famous tree, as does a bill from the Charter Oak Bank of Hartford (chartered by the state on August 22, 1853), a commemorative postage stamp, and numerous tokens and medals.

The U.S. Mint described the Charter Oak thus:

> If not for the famed "Charter Oak," Connecticut—and this country in general—might be a very different place than it is today! On the night of October 31, 1687, Connecticut's Charter was put to a test. A British representative for King James II challenged Connecticut's government structure and demanded its surrender. In the middle of the heated discussion, with the Charter on the table between the opposing parties, the candles were mysteriously snuffed out, darkening the room. When visibility was reestablished, the Connecticut Charter had vanished. Heroic Captain Joseph Wadsworth saved the Charter from the hands of the British and concealed it in the safest place he could find—in a majestic white oak.

The Robin and
the Mountain Laurel,
symbols of Connecticut

MINTAGE FIGURES

Circulation Coins (copper-nickel)	Proof Coins (copper-nickel)	Proof Coins (silver)
1999-P: 688,744,000 1999-D: 657,880,000	1999-S: 3,713,359	1999-S: 804,565

NUMISMATIC NOTES

Connecticut issued many types of currency during colonial times. The Higley threepence coins date from 1737 to 1739, struck from native metal in Granby. From 1785 to 1788 the young state issued its own copper coins. In the 19th century, Scovill Manufacturing Co., of Waterbury, was a major manufacturer of Hard Times tokens (struck during the economic hard times of the 1830s and 1840s), encased postage stamps (a substitute for pocket-change coins, which were hoarded during the Civil War by citizens fearful of a financial collapse), and Civil War tokens (private issues also intended to replace no-longer-circulating federal coins).

Two Commemoratives of the 1930s

The 1935 Connecticut Tercentenary half dollar honored the 300th anniversary of the state's original colonial charter. The 1936 Bridgeport half dollar commemorated that city's centennial.

Coins are shown enlarged.

MASSACHUSETTS

In February 1998 Governor Paul Cellucci began the process leading to the creation of a suitable coin design, and more than 100 youngsters provided sketches. Only children were invited—a novel approach and, so far, a unique one in the state quarter program. It would seem that the turnout was small. Perhaps it was not widely publicized. Otherwise, from aware youngsters in a state that values education, thousands of submissions would have been more likely.

6 of 50

Few states have more historical connections and design possibilities than Massachusetts. The Battle of Bunker Hill, Paul Revere and his famous ride, the Boston Tea Party, Cape Cod, and other scenarios come to mind. The design finally chosen for the state's quarter was a depiction of Daniel Chester French's famous *Minuteman* statue.

The statue is shown with a textured outline map of "The Bay State," complete with such details as Nantucket and Martha's Vineyard islands (among others) and a star indicating the location of Boston.

The Chickadee and the Mayflower, symbols of Massachusetts

MINTAGE FIGURES

Circulation Coins (copper-nickel)	Proof Coins (copper-nickel)	Proof Coins (silver)
2000-P: 628,600,000 2000-D: 535,184,000	2000-S: 4,020,172	2000-S: 965,421

NUMISMATIC NOTES

From 1652 to 1682 Massachusetts issued silver coins in the NE, Willow Tree, Oak Tree, and Pine Tree series, and in 1690 the colony issued the first paper money in the Western World. In 1787 and 1788 the state minted copper half cents and cents.

Various Massachusetts Colonial Coinage

Two Massachusetts-Related Commemoratives

Special half dollars were struck in 1920 and 1921 to mark the 300th anniversary of the landing of the Pilgrims at Plymouth. Another half dollar, minted in 1925, commemorated the battles of Lexington and Concord.

Some coins are shown enlarged.

MARYLAND

Numismatic author Q. David Bowers believes that Maryland "laid an egg with the design of this quarter dollar." He notes that the state wasted its "once-in-a-life-time coin opportunity" by honoring "the country's largest wooden dome built without nails."

A Mint news release gave these details:

7 of 50

Annapolis, March 13, 2000: In the Maryland State House Governor's Conference Room—an upstairs chamber decorated with portraits from Maryland's past—Governor Parris N. Glendening added a new contribution to the Old Line State's history. Before a group of onlookers, he unveiled the official Maryland state quarter in the very building the new coin honors. . . .

"In our view, the state house best favors Maryland's rich history, and the unique role the state has played in our nation's history," said Glendening.

George Washington is credited with coining the nickname of The Old Line State after the Battle of Long Island in August 1776. A line of Maryland troops held off the British while Washington retreated, with thousands of the soldiers killed in the action. After that, Washington referred to Maryland troops as "the old line"—always dependable.

The Baltimore Oriole and the Black-Eyed Susan, symbols of Maryland

MINTAGE FIGURES

Circulation Coins (copper-nickel)	Proof Coins (copper-nickel)	Proof Coins (silver)
2000-P: 678,200,000 2000-D: 556,532,000	2000-S: 4,020,172	2000-S: 965,421

NUMISMATIC NOTES

In 1658 and 1659, silver fourpence, sixpence, and shilling coins were struck at the Tower Mint in London, for circulation in Maryland. Colonial Maryland issued many types of currency. In 1783, Annapolis silversmith John Chalmers issued silver three-pence, sixpence, and shilling coins, and in 1790 Standish Barry, a Baltimore silversmith, issued a now-famous threepence coin. In the same era he produced a gold "doubloon" of Spanish-American design.

**1774 Maryland
Two-Thirds of
a Dollar Note**

This bill, issued in Annapolis, made a promise of payment to its bearer.

**1934 Maryland
Tercentenary Half Dollar**

This coin features a portrait of Cecil Calvert, Lord Baltimore, founder of the Maryland colony.

Note is shown reduced.

SOUTH CAROLINA

The South Carolina Numismatic Society was involved in picking the state's quarter design. The motif is among the most natural in the series, in terms of botany and zoology. The coin's flora and fauna, and the motto THE PAL-METTO STATE, overlap an outline map of South Carolina.

8 of 50

As Governor Jim Hodges described the design, "the Palmetto Tree represents South Carolina's strength; the Carolina Wren's song symbolizes the hospitality of the state's people; and the Yellow Jessamine, a delicate golden bloom—a sign of coming spring—is part of South Carolina's vast natural beauty."

The South Carolina state quarter's launch ceremony was held May 26, 2000. Jay Johnson, the director of the U.S. Mint, had been sworn into that office the day before, and this was his first public appearance in his new position. U.S. Treasurer Mary Ellen Withrow told the audience (at Dutch Fork Elementary School in Columbia): "Many of the ideas for the South Carolina quarter design came from elementary students who are enthusiastic about our nation's culture and history."

The Great Carolina Wren and the Yellow Jessamine, symbols of South Carolina

MINTAGE FIGURES

Circulation Coins (copper-nickel)	Proof Coins (copper-nickel)	Proof Coins (silver)
2000-P: 742,576,000 2000-D: 566,208,000	2000-S: 4,020,172	2000-S: 965,421

NUMISMATIC NOTES

South Carolina issued many types of currency during its colonial era.

1936 Columbia Sesquicentennial Half Dollar

A set of three half dollars was issued in 1936 to honor the 150-year anniversary of the capital city's founding.

Revolutionary War Soldiers

This scene shows men from various organizations in the Continental Army. Patriots of South Carolina, such as the soldier of the Second South Carolina Regiment (pictured in blue uniform in the background), would have used paper money issued by the former colony, as well as coins, tokens, and currency notes of the other soon-to-be states. (From a painting by Henry Alexander Ogden, published by the U.S. Army Quartermaster General in 1890)

NEW HAMPSHIRE

The Old Man of the Mountain, sometimes called the Great Stone Face, was a 40-foot rocky outcrop on Cannon Mountain in Franconia Notch. A longtime symbol of the state of New Hampshire, it had even attracted the attention of Daniel Webster, who wrote: "...up in the Mountains of New Hampshire, God Almighty has hung out a sign to show that here He makes

9 of 50

men." For years the tokens of the New Hampshire State Turnpike Commission pictured the famous landmark.

Q. David Bowers, who attended the launch ceremony, notes in *A Guide Book of Washington and State Quarters* that the new quarter has its own poem, "Common Coin," by New Hampshire poet laureate Marie Harris.

On May 3, 2003, the rocky Old Man of the Mountain tumbled down, the victim of thousands of years of weathering—warm summers alternating with icy winters. Less than three years after being minted, the New Hampshire state quarter had the unexpected and unwelcome distinction of being the first to show something that was in existence when the coin was struck, but now doesn't exist.

The Purple Finch and the Purple Lilac, symbols of New Hampshire

MINTAGE FIGURES

Circulation Coins (copper-nickel)	Proof Coins (copper-nickel)	Proof Coins (silver)
2000-P: 673,040,000 2000-D: 495,976,000	2000-S: 4,020,172	2000-S: 965,421

Numismatic Notes

New Hampshire issued its fair share of currency, of various types, during colonial times. In 1776, copper pattern coins were made there. Just one variety of Civil War token was issued in the state, by A.W. Gale of Concord, who operated a restaurant in the Concord railroad station.

**Vignette From a
New Hampshire Bank Note**

From 1792 to 1865, the state-chartered banks of New Hampshire were among the most sound in the nation, with very few that failed. This illustration of an Indian Princess is from a $5 note of the Strafford Bank in Dover.

1776 New Hampshire Copper Piece

New Hampshire was the first of the states to consider minting coins after the Declaration of Independence. "William Moulton was empowered to make a limited quantity of coins of pure copper…. Although cast patterns were prepared, it is believed that they were not approved. Little of the proposed coinage every circulated." (*A Guide Book of United States Coins*, 2007 edition)

VIRGINIA

A pleasing little flotilla of boats graces the center of the 2000 Virginia quarter—the *Susan Constant*, *Godspeed*, and *Discovery*—carrying brave emigrants on their way to what would become Jamestown, the first permanent English settlement in the New World. Under a charter granted to the Virginia Company by King James on April 10, 1606, the ves-

10 of 50

sels left London on September 20 of the same year. Nearly eight months later, the group of 104 men and boys landed on an island in the James River about 60 miles from the ocean. This was 13 years before the more famous arrival of the Pilgrims at Massachusetts far to the north. The Virginia quarter bears legends relating to the 400th anniversary of the event (an observance somewhat premature, but there were no complaints).

The mintage figures for Virginia quarters shattered all records, with 943,000,000 struck in Philadelphia and 651,616,000 in Denver. In 2004, writing in *Numismatic News*, Paul M. Green noted that the Philadelphia production by itself provided at least three Virginia quarters for every man, woman, and child in the nation!

The Cardinal and the Dogwood, symbols of Virginia

MINTAGE FIGURES

Circulation Coins (copper-nickel)	Proof Coins (copper-nickel)	Proof Coins (silver)
2000-P: 943,000,000 2000-D: 651,616,000	2000-S: 4,020,172	2000-S: 965,421

NUMISMATIC NOTES

Virginia issued many types of currency in colonial times. In 1773, in England, copper halfpence were struck for distribution in the colony. During the Civil War, Richmond was the capital of the Confederate States of America, and most CSA paper money bears its name. Many commemorative coins have honored the state and related themes: the year 1936 brought half dollars for the Lynchburg sesquicentennial, the Norfolk bicentennial, and the Roanoke Island 350th anniversary; a half dollar struck in 1937 remembered the Civil War's Battle of Antietam; and from 1946 to 1951, a run of half dollars honored Booker T. Washington. In more recent years, the George Washington half dollar was struck in 1982; the Bill of Rights silver dollar (featuring James Madison) was struck in 1993; and the Thomas Jefferson silver dollar was struck that same year. In 1999 one of the most attractive modern commemoratives was minted: the Dolley Madison silver dollar.

1999 Dolley Madison Silver Dollar

This commemorative coin honored the famous First Lady who rescued national treasures from the burning White House as the British invaded in the War of 1812. She and President Madison had a home in Virginia.

Coin is shown enlarged.

NEW YORK

It is not surprising to find the Statue of Liberty a major theme on New York's state quarter. The statue, standing on Liberty Island (formerly Bedloe's Island) in the harbor of New York City, is perhaps the most famous icon of America. It was officially dedicated on October 28, 1886, with President Grover Cleveland at the head of the ceremony. This

11 of 50

had been a long time coming. At the 1876 Centennial Exhibition in Philadelphia, Lady Liberty's detached, uplifted arm had been a great attraction, displaying part of the work in progress.

Other proposed designs for the quarter included Henry Hudson and his flagship *Half Moon*, a scene from the historical *Battle of Saratoga* painting, and the Federal Building on New York City's Wall Street. The Statue of Liberty claimed 76% of the ballots in a popularity vote.

At the quarter's launch ceremony, chocolate replicas were given away—possibly a numismatic collectible today, if they haven't all been eaten.

**The Bluebird
and the Rose,
symbols of New York**

MINTAGE FIGURES

Circulation Coins (copper-nickel)	Proof Coins (copper-nickel)	Proof Coins (silver)
2001-P: 655,400,000 2001-D: 619,640,000	2001-S: 3,094,140	2001-S: 889,697

NUMISMATIC NOTES

New York has a rich numismatic history dating to colonial times. In the 1780s, Nova Eborac and related copper coins were minted; Ephraim Brasher (a New York City goldsmith) made gold doubloons for local use; and Machin's Mills in Newburgh struck many counterfeit coins (including British halfpence) that circulated widely as change. In 1858, in New York City, the American Bank Note Co. became the world's largest currency printer, formed by consolidating eight firms. Many commemorative coins have had New York themes over the years: half dollars were struck for the Huguenot-Walloon Tercentenary in 1924; the Hudson Sesquicentennial in 1935; the Albany city charter's 250th anniversary in 1936; Long Island's 300th anniversary, also in 1936; and New Rochelle's 250th birthday, in 1938. In 2002, West Point's bicentennial was honored on a silver dollar.

Modern New York Commemoratives

The Statue of Liberty appeared on U.S. coins 15 years before the state quarter: half dollars, silver dollars, and $5 gold coins were struck in 1986.

NORTH CAROLINA

The 2001 North Carolina quarter depicts the Wright brothers' airplane that on December 17, 1903, flew a distance of 120 feet among the sand dunes of Kitty Hawk, on the seacoast of the state. Although S.P. Langley, backed by many assertions from the Smithsonian Institution, claimed that he was first in the manned flight of a self-propelled heavier-than-air machine, most historians have credited the Wrights. Perhaps the matter will never be resolved to everyone's satisfaction—sort of like who was the first to reach the North Pole, Cook or Peary?

12 of 50

The design is loosely adapted from a photograph by John P. Daniels, with Wilbur Wright standing in the foreground, watching the historic flight of his brother Orville lying flat on his stomach at the controls. (Concepts for the plane were developed and the craft constructed in Ohio, home of the Wright brothers, who operated a bicycle shop. Henry Ford, who collected all sorts of things, later bought the shop operated by the Wrights in Dayton, and moved it to Greenfield Village in Dearborn, Michigan, where it can be seen today.)

The Cardinal and
the American Dogwood,
symbols of North Carolina

MINTAGE FIGURES

Circulation Coins (copper-nickel)	Proof Coins (copper-nickel)	Proof Coins (silver)
2001-P: 627,600,000 2001-D: 427,876,000	2001-S: 3,094,140	2001-S: 889,697

NUMISMATIC NOTES

North Carolina produced many types of currency in its colonial days. In 1830 Christopher Bechtler (a German metallurgist) and family opened a private mint and assay office in Rutherfordton to coin $1.00, $2.50, and $5 gold pieces. They operated until 1852. From 1838 to 1861, the Charlotte Mint, a branch of the nation's main mint in Philadelphia, produced gold dollars, quarter eagles ($2.50 coins), and half eagles ($5 coins).

Gold Coins of North Carolina

Christopher Bechtler (pictured), his son August, and his nephew, Christopher Jr., struck their first gold dollars in 1831—nearly 20 years before the U.S. Mint made gold coins of that denomination. The Bechtlers' issues, like the "Five Dollars" piece pictured here, were well accepted by the public and circulated widely in the Southeast.

Coin is shown enlarged.

RHODE ISLAND

The Rhode Island quarter of 2001 is inscribed OCEAN STATE, reflecting the importance of the sea, including Narragansett Bay, a vast inlet of the Atlantic. The motif illustrates an old-fashioned sailboat gliding across the waves before the wind, evocative of the America's Cup races centered there for more than a half century. The coin's boat was mod-

13 of 50

eled after the *Reliance*, the 1903 winner of the America's Cup, a craft built in Bristol, Rhode Island, by the famous Herreshoff Manufacturing Co. In the distance is the Pell Bridge.

The official launch ceremony for the quarter dollar was held at Fort Adams State Park in Newport, a facility in active use as a fort from 1824 to 1850. Cannons fired and vintage yachts scooted around in the water offshore as part of a reenactment of the quarter design staged by the Rhode Island State Council on the Arts (RISCA).

With Rhode Island's quarter, each of the original 13 colonies were represented in the series.

The Rhode Island Red Hen and the Violet, symbols of Rhode Island

MINTAGE FIGURES

Circulation Coins (copper-nickel)	Proof Coins (copper-nickel)	Proof Coins (silver)
2001-P: 423,000,000 2001-D: 447,100,000	2001-S: 3,094,140	2001-S: 889,697

NUMISMATIC NOTES

Rhode Island issued many types of currency as a colony. From 1805 to 1809, the Farmers Exchange Bank of Gloucester issued large amounts of worthless paper money; it was the first major bank fraud in the United States. Many Civil War tokens of a distinctive style were issued in 1863 and 1864, mostly in Providence.

Rhode Island Ship Medal

Bearing the dates 1778 and 1779, the Rhode Island ship medals were struck (probably in England) as propaganda to influence Dutch policy during the American Revolution.

1936 Providence, Rhode Island, Tercentenary Half Dollar

A set of three commemorative half dollars (struck in Philadelphia, Denver, and San Francisco) was issued in 1936. They show a Native American welcoming Roger Williams, the founder of Providence, Rhode Island. (Strangely, the city's name is nowhere to be seen on the coin.)

Coin is shown enlarged.

VERMONT

14 of 50

Vermont's quarter features a scene of two maple trees in early spring, with sap buckets at the ready. Maple sugaring is in progress. Camel's Hump, the 4,083-foot landmark in the northern part of the Green Mountains range (from which the name *Vermont* was derived), forms the background.

Maple sugar production, earlier done by Native Americans, grew into an important industry in the state. The theme on the quarter offers a change from motifs earlier seen on Vermont-related coins, including the sun and forested ridge "landscape" design of Vermont's 1785–1786 copper pieces, and the Ira Allen/catamount design of the 1927 sesquicentennial commemorative half dollar.

The quarter's launch ceremony was a sweet one, with the Vermont Department of Agriculture selling sugar snow, maple cotton candy, maple creamies, and maple popcorn to benefit an education fund. Attendees with a sweet tooth received the new quarter in their change.

The Hermit Thrush and the Red Clover, symbols of Vermont

MINTAGE FIGURES

Circulation Coins (copper-nickel)	Proof Coins (copper-nickel)	Proof Coins (silver)
2001-P: 423,400,000 2001-D: 459,404,000	2001-S: 3,094,140	2001-S: 889,697

Numismatic Notes

An Act of April 14, 1781, authorized the issuance of paper money in Vermont, eventually amounting to £25,155 in total face value; these are rarities today. Vermont copper coins were struck in the late 1780s under contract at a private mint on Mill-brook, in Pawlet; and later at Machin's Mills, Newburgh, New York. The year 1806 saw the Vermont State Bank authorized—the first state-operated bank in the country.

1927 Vermont Sesquicentennial Half Dollar

This coin honored the 150th anniversary of the Battle of Bennington and the independence of Vermont.

Vermont Copper Coin of the 1780s

In 1785 and 1786, Vermont, independent and not yet a state, issued copper coins with the legend STELLA QUARTA DECIMA, or *The Fourteenth Star*. Vermont had hoped to achieve statehood by this time, but opposition from nearby New York (with which there were intense boundary disputes) blocked that goal. Finally, in 1791 Vermont became the 14th star in the flag, as its citizens had hoped.

KENTUCKY

The 2001 Kentucky quarter dollar illustrates a hilltop mansion with a thoroughbred racehorse behind a fence in the foreground. The United States Mint described the design:

15 of 50

> Kentucky was the first state on the western frontier to join the Union and is one of four states to call itself a "commonwealth." Kentucky is home of the longest running annual horse race in the country, the Kentucky Derby. The famous Kentucky bluegrass country is also grazing ground for some of the world's finest racehorses.

Also featured on the new quarter is another prominent symbol of Kentucky, Federal Hill, which has become known as My Old Kentucky Home. The design shows a side view of the famous Bardstown home where Stephen Foster wrote the state song, "My Old Kentucky Home."

The Cardinal and the Goldenrod, symbols of Kentucky

MINTAGE FIGURES

Circulation Coins (copper-nickel)	Proof Coins (copper-nickel)	Proof Coins (silver)
2001-P: 353,000,000 2001-D: 370,564,000	2001-S: 3,094,140	2001-S: 889,697

Numismatic NOTES

A British token of the 1790s, widely collected in America, is called the *Kentucky cent* or *Kentucky token* because it depicts a pyramid with 15 state abbreviations, with K, for Kentucky, at the top.

1790s Kentucky Token

1934–1938 Daniel Boone Bicentennial Half Dollar

Minted over the course of five years, these coins show the famous frontiersman with Chief Black Fish.

1796 P.P.P. Mydellton Token

These tokens, with inscriptions for the British Settlement [in] Kentucky, were related to a colonization scheme. They were made at the Soho Mint (Birmingham, England) from dies engraved by Conrad Küchler. Examples exist in copper and silver; all are rare.

Coin is shown enlarged.

TENNESSEE

The motif of the 2002 Tennessee quarter is a course in musical history of the state:

16 of 50

> The design incorporates musical instruments and a score with the inscription "Musical Heritage." Three stars represent Tennessee's three regions, and the instruments symbolize the distinct musical style of each region.
>
> The fiddle represents the Appalachian music of East Tennessee, the trumpet stands for the blues of West Tennessee for which Memphis is famous, and the guitar is for Central Tennessee, home to Nashville, the capital of country music. (from the U.S. Mint web site)

Writer Q. David Bowers notes that this coin has a design error: the guitar has six pegs, but only five strings! "Actually, there are six strings from the tuning pegs to the fretboard, but the sixth string disappears above the sound hole. There was some controversy about the details of the depicted trumpet, with the bell and leadpipe on the same side as the valves. The same error is on the 2002 Louisiana quarter. Errors in design details contribute to the enjoyment of numismatics and are always amusing to contemplate."

The coin's launch ceremony was held in Nashville at the Ford Motor Company Theatre at the Country Music Hall of Fame. Famous country singer Ricky Skaggs was among the entertainers.

The Mockingbird and the Iris, symbols of Tennessee

MINTAGE FIGURES

Circulation Coins (copper-nickel)	Proof Coins (copper-nickel)	Proof Coins (silver)
2002-P: 361,600,000 2002-D: 286,468,000	2002-S: 3,084,245	2002-S: 892,229

NUMISMATICNOTES

Several Tennessee merchants issued Civil War tokens in the 1860s. Today these tokens, struck as substitutes for regular coins (which were hoarded by people nervous about the nation's economic future), range from scarce to rare.

A Scene From the War in East Tennessee, Oct 1863

"Reception of General Burnside by the Unionists of Knoxville" (from _Harper's Weekly_, October 24, 1863).

OHIO

Ohio's quarter honors the state's contribution to the fields of aviation and aeronautics. Both Neil Armstrong and John Glenn were born in Ohio, as was Orville Wright, co-inventor of the airplane. The Wright brothers' 1905 *Flyer III*, one of their early aircraft, was built and tested there.

The original design legend, BIRTHPLACE OF AVIATION, was changed to BIRTHPLACE OF AVIATION PIONEERS. The Commission of Fine Arts recommended the change, given the question of where aviation was actually "born" (the first flight took place in North Carolina, which had already depicted the Wright brothers on its state quarter). Furthermore, aviation could be dated back more than a century, to early lighter-than-air balloons.

The coin's launch ceremony was held at the United States Air Force Museum at Wright-Patterson Air Force Base. Adjacent to the museum is Huffman Prairie Flying Field, where the Wright brothers mastered their craft in 1904 and 1905. John Glenn (space pioneer and U.S. senator) was on hand, as was Neil Armstrong, the first person to set foot on the moon.

Commenting on North Carolina and Ohio, and their competing Wright brothers designs, Armstrong said during the ceremony, "Both states can take justifiable pride: Ohio had the intellect and North Carolina had the wind."

The Cardinal and the Scarlet Carnation, symbols of Ohio

MINTAGE FIGURES

Circulation Coins (copper-nickel)	Proof Coins (copper-nickel)	Proof Coins (silver)
2002-P: 217,200,000 2002-D: 414,832,000	2002-S: 3,084,245	2002-S: 892,229

NUMISMATIC NOTES

In 1916 and 1917, commemorative gold dollars were struck for the McKinley Memorial. In 1922, both half dollars and gold dollars were minted for the Ulysses S. Grant Memorial. In 1936, commemorative half dollars were struck for the Cincinnati Musical Center and for the centennial of the city of Cleveland. Sidney, Ohio, was the birthplace of the hobby newspaper *Coin World* in 1960.

A Montage of Ohio-Related Commemoratives

Some coins are shown enlarged.

LOUISIANA

The textured area of the 2002 Louisiana state quarter represents the land of the Louisiana Purchase in relation to the rest of the mainland United States. This famous acquisition was made in 1803, President Thomas Jefferson's record-setting addition to the national territory—at the modest cost of $15 million, or about 3¢ per acre. The brown pelican,

18 of 50

the state bird of Louisiana, is also featured on the quarter, as are a trumpet and several musical notes, honoring the tradition of jazz in New Orleans.

The state's design selection process began when Governor Mike Foster set up the Louisiana Commemorative Coin Advisory Commission, charged with finding a design "easily understood by both the youth of the state of Louisiana and the youth of other states." The Commission reviewed 1,193 design suggestions, about 80% of which were submitted by schoolchildren.

The Eastern Brown Pelican and the Magnolia, symbols of Louisiana

MINTAGE FIGURES

Circulation Coins (copper-nickel)	Proof Coins (copper-nickel)	Proof Coins (silver)
2002-P: 362,000,000 2002-D: 402,204,000	2002-S: 3,084,245	2002-S: 892,229

NUMISMATIC NOTES

Among coin collectors, Louisiana is famous for the New Orleans Mint, opened in 1838; it continued coinage until being closed down during the Civil War (1861), then reopened in 1879, continuing its operations until 1909.

Louisiana DIX Note

Numismatic historian Q. David Bowers observes that certain $10 notes were issued in New Orleans in the 1830s, imprinted DIX (*ten* in French). He believes these were the inspiration for reference to the "land of dixes," or *Dixie*. The story of the DIX note is told in *The 100 Greatest American Currency Notes* (Bowers/Sundman, 2006).

Note is shown reduced.

INDIANA

The Indiana quarter of 2000 includes 19 stars as part of its design. The primary images are an outline map of the state and a racecar—one of the kind used in the famous Indianapolis 500 races, held every year since 1911 except during the world wars. The angled and dynamic car appears to almost be speeding toward the viewer, one of the

19 of 50

most active visual effects on any state quarter. One might argue there was a violation of the Mint rule against showing commercial interests in the designs: the Indy 500 is a privately owned enterprise. The inscription CROSSROADS OF AMERICA reflects the status of the state as a focus of transportation.

Design ideas were gathered starting at the Indiana State Fair on August 17, 1999. Eventually 3,737 ideas were received by the Indiana Quarter Design Committee. The governor's office, in a May 5, 2000, press release, described some of the other major themes: the state outline with a cardinal superimposed; the torch and stars from the state flag; a basketball player.

**The Cardinal
and the Peony,
symbols of Indiana**

MINTAGE FIGURES

Circulation Coins (copper-nickel)	Proof Coins (copper-nickel)	Proof Coins (silver)
2002-P: 362,600,000 2002-D: 327,200,000	2002-S: 3,084,245	2002-S: 892,229

Numismatic Notes

In the late 1830s a *Hoosier tame cat* was the nickname for an often-worthless bank note from Indiana. Later, the state developed a well-organized banking system; Hugh McCulloch, a major force in that effort, later became the first comptroller of the currency for the United States Treasury.

Hugh McCulloch

McCulloch, the "Father of Modern Banking," served as Secretary of the Treasury under three American presidents: Abraham Lincoln, Andrew Johnson, and Chester A. Arthur. He was present in the Petersen boarding-house room as President Lincoln lay dying. McCulloch became an intimate advisor to Lincoln's successor, Andrew Johnson, and was influential in the federal government in the tempestuous months following the assassination.

MISSISSIPPI

The Mississippi quarter of 2002, with its bold treatment, is simple and effective in its concept, reflecting a tried-and-true symbol in the state flower. The depiction of *Magnolia grandiflora* scored an artistic success.

20 of 50

The motif is unusual in that the magnolia is both the state tree (made official on April 1, 1938, by vote of the state legislature) and the state flower (as of February 26, 1952). The magnolia is not native, but was introduced from Asia. Its name is derived from Pierre Magnol, a French botanist.

Virtually nothing was publicized nationally about the creation process of the coin's design.

MINTAGE FIGURES

Circulation Coins (copper-nickel)	Proof Coins (copper-nickel)	Proof Coins (silver)
2002-P: 290,000,000 2002-D: 289,600,000	2002-S: 3,084,245	2002-S: 892,229

**The Mockingbird
and the Magnolia,
symbols of Mississippi**

NUMISMATIC NOTES

In 1862, during the Civil War siege of Vicksburg, copper-nickel Indian Head cents were counterstamped and used as 10-cent pieces.

Victors of the Siege of Vicksburg

Pictured are Major-General McPherson, of Grant's army, and his chief engineers (from a sketch by Mr. Theo. R. Davis, in *Harper's Weekly*, August 1, 1863).

Settling the Terms of Surrender

Harper's illustrated an interview between generals Grant and Pemberton (*Harper's Weekly*, August 1, 1863).

ILLINOIS

In January 2001 the Governor's Classroom Contest encouraged young citizens of Illinois to submit their ideas for the quarter. Eventually more than 6,000 concepts were submitted, about 95% of them from schoolchildren. A 14-person committee then reviewed the suggestions and narrowed them down to three categories: state history, agriculture

21 of 50

and industry, and symbols of Illinois. The U.S. Mint created five different designs from these, from which Governor George Ryan made the final decision.

An outline map of Illinois sets the background for the design of the state's 2003 quarter. A standing portrait of Abraham Lincoln as a young man, inspired by the statue *The Resolute Lincoln*, is seen inside the map, while other motifs emphasize the state's urban and rural agricultural diversity. Around the border are 21 stars, reflecting the state's sequence in joining the Union on December 3, 1818.

On Monday, January 6, 2003, the launch ceremony was held at the James R. Thompson Center in Chicago. Mint Director Henrietta Holsman Fore, a frequent and popular attendee to such launches (a few other times she sent a deputy director), led the event, with state First Lady Lura Lynn Ryan at her side. Music was provided by the Lake Bluff Middle School Choir.

The Cardinal and the Purple Violet, symbols of Illinois

Mintage Figures

Circulation Coins (copper-nickel)	Proof Coins (copper-nickel)	Proof Coins (silver)
2003-P: 225,800,000 2003-D: 237,400,000	2003-S: 3,408,516	2003-S: 1,125,755

Numismatic Notes

The American Numismatic Association was formed at an 1891 meeting in Chicago. It continues as the hobby's most important organization today (learn more about the ANA at www.money.org). Another Illinois claim to numismatic fame is the issue of the United States' first commemorative coins, struck for the World's Columbian Exposition, held in Chicago. Half dollars were struck in 1892 and 1893, and the Isabella quarter dollar in 1893. Twenty-five years later, in 1918, the Illinois Centennial commemorative half dollar would feature a profile portrait of Abraham Lincoln. In 1936 a half dollar honored the centennial of Elgin, Illinois.

1918 Illinois Centennial Half Dollar

This was the first United States half dollar issued to commemorate a state's centennial. The reverse design is based on the state seal.

Coin is shown enlarged.

ALABAMA

The Alabama state quarter features Helen Keller (1880–1968), author, lecturer, and college graduate (with honors), who had lost her sight, hearing, and speech from illness at the tender age of 19 months. Alexander Graham Bell helped form a relationship between the Keller family Anne Sullivan, who taught Helen to communicate and worked with her

22 of 50

for 50 years. The play and movie) *Miracle Worker* is based on their partnership. The coin features Keller's name in English as well as in Braille. At the sides are a long-leaf pine branch and flowers, while a banner inscribed SPIRIT OF COURAGE symbolizes Keller's life.

Q. David Bowers describes the reaction to the coin's design:

> The use of Keller as a motif was unexpected to many citizens, who did not consider her to be a recognizable icon to represent the state. This was no reflection on her accomplishments. Many numismatists expressed the same surprise. About the flowers, the Mint calls this part of the design a *magnolia* branch, per a letter of April 27, 2001, from Governor Don Siegelman. However, six professors of horticulture at the College of Agriculture at Auburn University stated that, in fact, *red camellias* were depicted—not a surprise, since the camellia is the state flower, and Alabama is known as the Camellia State.

The Yellowhammer and the Camellia, symbols of Alabama

MINTAGE FIGURES

Circulation Coins (copper-nickel)	Proof Coins (copper-nickel)	Proof Coins (silver)
2003-P: 225,000,000 2003-D: 232,400,000	2003-S: 3,408,516	2003-S: 1,125,755

NUMISMATIC NOTES

Montgomery, Alabama, was the first capital of the Confederacy. "Montgomery Notes" of $50, $100, $500, and $1,000 bear this imprint. In the 1860s, White & Swann, merchants in Huntsville, issued Civil War tokens. Alabama Centennial commemorative half dollars were issued in 1921 (two years after the state's actual centennial).

1921 Alabama Centennial Half Dollar

This coin shows the portraits of William Wyatt Bibb (the first governor of Alabama) and T.E. Kilby (governor at the time of the state's centennial). This was the first United States coin to feature a living person.

Coin is shown enlarged.

MAINE

The Maine quarter of 2003 was the last for the six states of New England. Maine became a state on March 15, 1820, under the Missouri Compromise—the "balancing" of the Union by adding a state with freedom, to match the slaveholding state of Missouri. Before that, Maine was a district of Massachusetts, separated from that state by New Hampshire.

23 of 50

More than 100,000 citizens voted on several proposed Maine sketches (narrowed down from 600 entries), and the Pemaquid Point Lighthouse was the most popular. Daniel J. Carr, a Colorado artist, submitted the design. The motif was created in cooperation with Leland and Carolyn Pendleton of Rockland, Maine, the coastal port home of the three-masted schooner *Victory Chimes* (also pictured on the coin). This was done to satisfy the rule that the motif must be by a Maine resident. Q. David Bowers describes the coin as "a splendid blending of Carr's talent with the artistry of Mint engraver-sculptor Donna Weaver."

Maine's launch ceremony featured a sweet souvenir: Wilbur's of Maine Chocolate Confections contributed silver-foil-wrapped chocolate replicas at the ceremony held at the Lighthouse, June 2, 2003.

The Chickadee and the White Pine Cone and Tassel, symbols of Maine

MINTAGE FIGURES

Circulation Coins (copper-nickel)	Proof Coins (copper-nickel)	Proof Coins (silver)
2003-P: 217,400,000 2003-D: 231,400,000	2003-S: 3,408,516	2003-S: 1,125,755

NUMISMATIC NOTES

After Maine became a separate state, banks that had been issuing currency with the Massachusetts imprint afterward issued Maine notes. Maine's new status created banks that were located first in one state, then in another, but which did not move an inch! In 1840 the famous Castine hoard of coins was found. During the Civil War, just one Maine merchant issued Civil War tokens, R.S. Torrey, inventor of the Maine State Bee Hive. Two commemorative half dollars were struck with Maine themes, for the 1920 Maine Centennial, and the 1936 York County Tercentenary.

Maine Civil War Token

Massachusetts Pine Tree Shillings in Maine

From November 1840 through April 1841, Captain Stephen Grindle and his son Samuel unearthed hundreds of silver coins on their farm near the harbor of Castine, Maine. The coins are believed to have been buried around 1690. Many Massachusetts Pine Tree shillings and related pieces were found. *The Guide Book of United States Coins* describes the hoard as one of the most famous in American history.

Token is shown enlarged.

MISSOURI

24 of 50

Missouri's quarter design brought a controversy to the program. A statewide competition brought about 3,300 submissions. From these, a dozen semi-finalists were chosen and posted on the Internet for voting. About 175,000 responses were received. Finally, a sketch was selected that featured the Lewis and Clark expedition, by Paul Jackson, a Missouri artist. Jackson later accused the U.S. Mint of grossly modifying his design without consultation, and publicly protested the changes, including on National Public Radio. Eventually the brouhaha involved the Commission of Fine Arts, the Mint, and the public and numismatic press. Hobby historian Q. David Bowers writes:

> The affair was a first-class headache for just about everyone involved, creating a quarter that many observers found to be one of the poorest motifs so far in the series. Mint Director Jay Johnson later reminisced, "I still remember the remark that the design looked like three men in a tub rowing between two clumps of broccoli!"

The Bluebird and the Hawthorn, symbols of Missouri

This regrettable controversy was the catalyst for the United States Mint revising its rules. Future quarter designs would be created by the Mint itself—no outside talent wanted. Instead, concepts were to be submitted in writing, and the Mint would do the artistry.

MINTAGE FIGURES

Circulation Coins (copper-nickel)	Proof Coins (copper-nickel)	Proof Coins (silver)
2003-P: 225,000,000 2003-D: 228,200,000	2003-S: 3,408,516	2003-S: 1,125,755

NUMISMATIC NOTES

St. Louis World's Fair Gold Dollars

In 1904 the Louisiana Purchase Exposition (St. Louis World's Fair) saw the issuance of commemorative gold dollars dated 1903, one with the recently assassinated William McKinley and the other with Thomas Jefferson. In 1921 Missouri's centennial was honored with a commemorative half dollar.

Westward Journey Nickels

"While the Missouri quarter garnered scarcely any praise or admiration, it became part of the series…. If it is any consolation to Missourians, a few years later the 2004 Westward Journey nickel series focusing on Lewis and Clark drew unstinted praise from just about everyone." (Bowers, *A Guide Book of Washington and State Quarters*)

ARKANSAS

The Arkansas quarter of 2003 features a collage of items relating to the state. The U.S. Mint described the design on its web site:

25 of 50

> It is fitting that the "Natural State," Arkansas's official nickname, chose images of natural resources. Arkansas has an abundance of clear streams, rivers and lakes. In fact, Arkansas has more than 600,000 acres of natural lakes. Arkansas is also known for its sportsmanship and boasts mallard hunting as a main attraction for hunters across the nation.

Visitors to Arkansas can search Crater of Diamonds State Park for precious gems including, of course, diamonds. The mine at Crater of Diamonds State Park reportedly is the oldest diamond mine in North America, and the only one in the United States open to the public. Visitors get to keep what they find.

Visitors can also experience "rice fever" in Arkansas—just the way W.H. Fuller did when he grew the first commercially successful rice crop in Arkansas. Soon after, thousands of acres of the Grand Prairie were changed to cultivate rice, and Arkansas became the leading producer of the grain in the United States.

The Mockingbird and the Apple Blossom, symbols of Arkansas

MINTAGE FIGURES

Circulation Coins (copper-nickel)	Proof Coins (copper-nickel)	Proof Coins (silver)
2003-P: 228,000,000 2003-D: 229,800,000	2003-S: 3,408,516	2003-S: 1,125,755

NUMISMATIC NOTES

From 1935 to 1939, the U.S. Mint struck half dollars honoring Arkansas' centennial.

The Arkansas Centennial half dollar portrays an Indian chief of 1836 (the year Arkansas became a state) and an American girl of 1936, wearing a Liberty cap. In 1936, Senator Joseph Robinson received a rare honor: though still living, his portrait was featured in a second reverse design for the coin.

Coins are shown enlarged.

MICHIGAN

Governor John Engler established the Michigan Quarter Commission in November 2001, with 25 members, including numismatists. Residents of the state were encouraged to submit ideas, and 4,300 were received.

In September 2003, Governor Jennifer Granholm, in consultation with designer Stephen M. Bieda, selected the winner, a motif

26 of 50

similar in concept to the Cleveland Centennial commemorative half dollar of 1936, with outline maps of the five Great Lakes as the central theme. (Michigan borders on four of these lakes; per a Mint release, "standing anywhere in the state, a person is within 85 miles of one of the Great Lakes.")

The final design engendered quite a bit of controversy, both in numismatic periodicals and in Michigan newspapers. Among various state designs, it seemed to be among the least pleasing to many people, since it failed to symbolize any achievements, famous people, or scenic depiction of the state. By this time, critiquing the designs had become a pastime for many citizens, including coin collectors—quite unlike at the start of the program, when just about everyone admired the 1999 Delaware quarter.

The Robin and the Apple Blossom, symbols of Michigan

MINTAGE FIGURES

Circulation Coins (copper-nickel)	Proof Coins (copper-nickel)	Proof Coins (silver)
2004-P: 233,800,000 2004-D: 225,800,000	2004-S: 2,761,163	2004-S: 1,789,344

NUMISMATIC NOTES

During the Civil War, many Michigan merchants in Detroit and elsewhere issued Civil War tokens. In 1888, George F. Heath of Monroe launched *The Numismatist*, later to become the official magazine of the American Numismatic Association.

1836 Gobrecht Dollar

In 1836, the Gobrecht silver dollar featured 26 stars on its reverse, in anticipation of Michigan's becoming the 26th state. This was the first U.S. silver dollar minted since 1804.

1864 Michigan Civil War Token

A Civil War token issued by W. Darling of Saranac, Michigan, in 1864 is worth between $7,500 (in Very Good condition) and $15,000 (in About Uncirculated) condition.

Token is shown enlarged.

FLORIDA

Florida Governor Jeb Bush appointed the Florida Commemorative Quarter Committee on April 9, 2002. Gary E. Lewis, a collector from Cape Coral, was its chairman; he would later serve as president of the American Numismatic Association, 2003 to 2005.

27 of 50

The committee narrowed more than 1,500 ideas down to 10, and the governor selected five semi-finalists: "The Everglades," "Gateway to Discovery," "Fishing Capital of the World," "St. Augustine," and "America's Spaceport." The final choice was put to the vote of the citizens. Q. David Bowers describes the chosen "Gateway to Discovery" design:

> The main reason Spanish galleons are associated with the state is that centuries ago the Spanish treasure fleet, typically consisting of a dozen or more vessels, returned from possessions in the New World, bearing gold and silver coins and ingots for the royal coffers. The typical homeward route called for a rendezvous at Havana, then passage northward along the east coast of Florida, then into the broad Atlantic. During the hurricane season, certain of these ships perished on the shoals and beaches of Florida, including virtually the entire fleets of 1715 and 1733. Many coins have been recovered from the remains of these vessels, to the delight of the collecting community.

The Mockingbird and the Orange Blossom, symbols of Florida

MINTAGE FIGURES

Circulation Coins (copper-nickel)	Proof Coins (copper-nickel)	Proof Coins (silver)
2004-P: 240,200,000 2004-D: 241,600,000	2004-S: 2,761,163	2004-S: 1,789,344

NUMISMATIC NOTES

The East Coast of Florida and the Florida Keys have yielded many silver and gold coins sunk since fleets of Spanish galleons encountered hurricanes in the 18th century. Florida United Numismatists (FUN) was established in 1955; today it is perhaps the strongest state numismatic club, and thousands of collectors attend its FUN Show held every year in January.

Examining Coins From the Wreck of the *Atocha*

In 1986 Ken Bressett, editor of the *Guide Book of United States Coins* (the "Red Book") dove for treasure with Mel Fisher, exploring the wreck of the Spanish galleon *Atocha* off Florida's coast.

1935 Old Spanish Trail Half Dollar (Reverse)

In 1935, the route depicted on the map on the Old Spanish Trail commemorative half dollar began in Florida.

Coin is shown enlarged.

TEXAS

The Republic of Texas, which had used the lone star emblem on its flag beginning in 1839, joined the Union as the 28th state in 1845. Its state quarter reflects this history with an outline map, a large single star, and the inscription THE LONE STAR STATE.

28 of 50

The state name is derived from *Tejas*, an Indian word meaning "friends," a logical connection to its present-day motto, *Friendship*.

In August 2000, Governor George W. Bush appointed the Texas Quarter Dollar Coin Advisory Committee. This group enlisted the Texas Numismatic Association to supervise a contest which resulted in more than 2,500 ideas submitted, these only from natives of the state or those who had lived there for at least a year as of May 11, 2001. Governor Rick Perry selected the winner, a sketch made by Daniel Miller, a graphic artist from Arlington, who said, "My objective was to create something big and bold … I think what really inspired me was the Texas flag." He meant the *current* state banner, of course; over the centuries, the district has been under the flags of Spain, France, Mexico, the Republic of Texas, the United States of America, the Confederate States of America, and the U.S.A. again—six different.

The Mockingbird and the Bluebonnet, symbols of Texas

MINTAGE FIGURES

Circulation Coins (copper-nickel)	Proof Coins (copper-nickel)	Proof Coins (silver)
2004-P: 278,800,000 2004-D: 263,000,000	2004-S: 2,761,163	2004-S: 1,789,344

NumismaticNOTES

The Republic of Texas, formed in 1836, issued its own paper money. In 1900, Texan B. Max Mehl (1884–1957) started in the rare coin business; in time he would become America's most famous dealer. Texas Centennial commemorative half dollars were minted from 1934 to 1938. Another half dollar, from 1935, honored the Old Spanish Trail.

1935 Texas Independence
Centennial Half Dollar

The reverse of this commemorative shows portraits of General Sam Houston and Stephen Austin, founders of the Republic and State of Texas.

1935 Old Spanish Trail
Half Dollar (Obverse)

This coin commemorated the 400th anniversary of the overland expedition of Alvar Nuñez Cabeza de Vaca through the American gulf area. The obverse design is explained by the English translation of the explorer's name: "Cow's Head." His journey began in Florida and ended in what would become Texas.

Some coins are shown enlarged.

IOWA

The Iowa Commemorative Quarter Commission included two numismatists: Tom Robertson and Brian Fanton. Libraries, banks, and credit unions were used to gather the 5,000 designs submitted by Iowa citizens. These were narrowed down by the Commission to "American Gothic," "Foundation in Education," "Feeding the World," "Sullivan Brothers," and "Beautiful Land."

29 of 50

The theme of the five Sullivan brothers of Waterloo (who died heroically in November 1942 when their ship, the U.S.S. *Juneau*, was sunk) drew some fire from critics who said that certain of the brothers were juvenile delinquents before they went into military service. "Feeding the World" tied in with the state's corn production. *American Gothic*, of course, is Grant Wood's famous painting of a solemn-visaged farm couple, embodying agriculture and hard work. Governor Vilsack finally chose "Foundation in Education" as the theme. The final design (inspired by another Grant Wood painting, *Arbor Day*), shows a group of schoolchildren and a teacher planting a tree.

The Eastern Goldfinch and the Wild Prairie Rose, symbols of Iowa

MINTAGE FIGURES

Circulation Coins (copper-nickel)	Proof Coins (copper-nickel)	Proof Coins (silver)
2004-P: 213,800,000 2004-D: 251,400,000	2004-S: 2,761,163	2004-S: 1,789,344

NUMISMATIC NOTES

In 1863, First National Bank of Davenport was the first National Bank to open its doors for business.

(State emblem from *A Centennial View of our Country and its Resources*, 1876)

1946 Iowa Centennial Half Dollar

Just over 100,000 coins were struck of this commemorative, described by the *Guide Book of United States Coins*: "The reverse shows the Iowa state seal, and the obverse shows the first stone capitol building at Iowa City. This issue was sold to the residents of Iowa and only a small remainder to others. Nearly all of the issue was disposed of within several months, except for some that were held back by the state for sale at future anniversary dates."

Coin is shown enlarged.

WISCONSIN

30 of 50

In December 2001 Governor Scott McCallum named 23 people to the Wisconsin Commemorative Quarter Council. Some 9,608 ideas were submitted (mostly from schoolchildren), which the committee narrowed to six. These were further reduced by a statewide referendum to three, including "Scenic Wisconsin" and "Early Exploration and Cultural Interaction." A third, "Agriculture/Dairy/Barns" was the people's choice.

The Wisconsin quarter features the head of a cow and a wheel of cheese echoing the state motto, "America's Dairyland" (not used on the coin, though another motto, FORWARD, was). An ear of corn was also depicted, possibly making Iowans jealous!

The launch ceremony was held on October 25, 2004, at a facility in State Fair Park in West Allis. An estimated 5,000 people were on hand. Children were given free quarters, and adults could buy them for face value. Governor Doyle commented that one cow, such as shown on the quarter, creates $15,000 to $17,000 worth of economic activity.

The first "gold rush" in the state quarter series occurred in January 2005, when word spread of two curious die varieties discovered among 2004-D (struck in Denver) Wisconsin quarters. These are the only varieties among state quarters that have thus far captured the fancy of thousands of collectors.

The Robin and the Wood Violet, symbols of Wisconsin

The coins have two distinct variations on the reverse. The *Guide Book of United States Coins* calls them "Extra Leaf High" (in which an extra leaf appears on the ear of corn on the reverse) and "Extra Leaf Low" (the same, but positioned slightly lower than the other variety). The varieties were first reported in Tucson, Arizona.

Sets of these odd coins have sold for hundreds, and even *thousands*, of dollars! Check your pocket change carefully... you might have one of these special quarters.

MINTAGE FIGURES

Circulation Coins (copper-nickel)	Proof Coins (copper-nickel)	Proof Coins (silver)
2004-P: 226,400,000 2004-D: 226,800,000	2004-S: 2,761,163	2004-S: 1,789,344

NUMISMATIC NOTES

In 1863, Wisconsin merchants were important issuers of Civil War tokens. The year 1936 brought the Wisconsin Territorial Centennial commemorative half dollar. *Numismatic News* was founded in 1952 by collector Chester Krause, in Iola; from his hard work would grow the hobby giant Krause Publications.

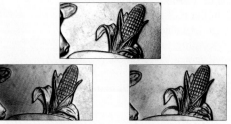

Wisconsin Quarter Varieties
The normal-die reverse is shown at top. The Extra Leaf High and Extra Leaf Low varieties are shown in the second row, at left and right.

Shown enlarged.

CALIFORNIA

Although the Mint's new rules prohibited states from submitting sketches beginning with the 2005 coins, they made an exception for California. The 20 top concepts were presented in an Internet poll and whittled down to five. Popular sentiment had the Gold Rush motif as the front runner, but Governor Arnold Schwarzenegger surprised everyone and picked the

31 of 50

John Muir / Yosemite National Park theme. The Sierra Club had supported and campaigned vigorously for Garrett Burke's highly artistic design, a fact that had the Gold Rush supporters crying foul when the announcement was made. Regardless of disappointments and protests, the result is one of the most aesthetically pleasing designs in the series.

Released on January 31, 2005, the coin features the standing figure of John Muir with a scene of Yosemite National Park's Half Dome in the background. A California condor, an endangered species, flies overhead. According to the governor, he made the final choice based on the beauty and significance of the design. John Muir inspired generations of Californians to preserve the natural beauty of the state.

The California Valley Quail and the Golden Poppy, symbols of California

MINTAGE FIGURES

Circulation Coins (copper-nickel)	Proof Coins (copper-nickel)	Proof Coins (silver)
2005-P: 257,200,000 2005-D: 263,200,000	2005-S: 3,262,000	2005-S: 1,606,970

NUMISMATIC NOTES

The discovery of gold at Sutter's Mill on January 24, 1848, was the catalyst for California's Gold Rush. Many private gold coins were minted from 1849 to 1855, and federal assay offices produced gold ingots. Finally, in 1854, the San Francisco Mint was opened. Many commemorative coins have honored California themes over the years: the Panama-Pacific International Exposition (five coins minted in 1915); the Monroe Doctrine Centennial (1923); the California Diamond Jubilee (1925); the San Diego California Pacific Exposition (1935–1936); the San Francisco–Oakland Bay Bridge (1936); and the Los Angeles Olympic Games (1983–1984).

A Montage of California-Related Commemoratives

MINNESOTA

32 of 50

The Minnesota quarter features an idyllic lake scene. Two people fish from a small boat between a loon in the foreground and a tree-lined shore in the background. A tex-tured outline of the state is depicted to the side of the boat bearing the state nickname, "Land of 10,000 Lakes."

Minnesota sent five design concepts to the U.S. Mint. Of those, the Mint provided four renderings (one was discarded). Three of the four included a loon and two included a lake. These drawings were put on display at the Mall of America for public review and comment, and the final design choice sparked no controversy.

The quarter was launched in the morning of April 12, 2005, at the State Capitol building in St. Paul. Free quarters were given to those 18 and younger, and adults could buy them for face value. Sports stars Kent Hrbek from the Minnesota Twins and Ed McDaniel from the Minnesota Vikings were on hand. Music was provided by the Lakeville High School Band, the Nativez Inc. drummers, and the Minnesota Boys Choir.

Certain copper-nickel Proof Minnesota quarters have a die break running from the top of Washington's head to the border. These are nicknamed the "Spike Head" variety. Check your Proof sets; these coins have an additional value.

The Common Loon and the Pink and White Lady's-Slipper, symbols of Minnesota

MINTAGE FIGURES

Circulation Coins (copper-nickel)	Proof Coins (copper-nickel)	Proof Coins (silver)
2005-P: 239,600,000 2005-D: 248,400,000	2005-S: 3,262,000	2005-S: 1,606,970

NUMISMATIC NOTES

This token, issued by a druggist in Winona, is worth $600 in Very Fine condition or $1,500 in Mint State–63. The typical Minnesota Civil War token "store card" is worth $450 or $750 in those grades. A store card is a tradesman's token, privately struck during the war. These circulated as substitutes for regular coins, which were widely hoarded. According to the *Guide Book of United States Coins*, "An estimated 50,000,000 or more of these pieces were issued. Approximately 10,000 different varieties have been recorded." Some store cards bore promises that they could be exchanged for goods (e.g., "Good for one cigar," "Good for one drink"); others, like the druggist's token show here, simply advertised a business. Private manufacturers minted these tokens at a cost of less than a penny apiece, then put them into circulation as substitutes for the same-sized Indian Head cent (pictured), keeping the profit.

Civil War Token from Minnesota

Token and coin are shown enlarged.

OREGON

Oregon's coin is another that focuses on a natural resource—Crater Lake, which is the deepest lake in America at 1,949 feet. The coin depicts a panorama of Crater Lake shown from the southern rim. Pine trees are in the foreground and on the shore, while Wizard Island rises from the water.

33 of 50

The 18-member Oregon Commemorative Coin Commission weeded through the many suggestions entered and chose the Crater Lake concept by a narrow margin. The final choice went to the governor, who endorsed the selection. The U.S. Mint quickly approved the design.

The launch ceremony was held at the Oregon Historical Society in Portland on June 15, 2005. The ceremony featured representatives from three Oregon Native American tribes. An ice-cream party followed where coins were free for kids and available for face value to older folks.

The design is widely appreciated by numismatists as one of the finest in the series. The elements each contribute to a main scene, rather than floating randomly in a montage, giving artistic value to the motif.

The Western Meadowlark and the Oregon Grape, symbols of Oregon

MINTAGE FIGURES

Circulation Coins (copper-nickel)	Proof Coins (copper-nickel)	Proof Coins (silver)
2005-P: 316,200,000 2005-D: 404,000,000	2005-S: 3,262,000	2005-S: 1,606,970

NUMISMATIC NOTES

In 1845, the name of an Oregon settlement was decided by the toss of a coin: settler Asa Lovejoy (from Massachusetts) preferred *Boston*, and Francis Pettygrove (from Maine) wanted *Portland*. The coin they flipped was an 1835 large cent—and Pettygrove won the toss. In 1849, the Oregon Exchange Co. minted $5 and $10 gold coins. On July 4, 1864, Congress passed "An Act to establish a Branch Mint of the United States at Dalles City in the state of Oregon for the coinage of gold and silver." $100,000 was appropriated. A fine mint building was constructed, but never used. In 1904 and 1905, commemorative gold dollars were issued for the Lewis and Clark Exposition in Portland. From 1926 to 1939, the Mint issued a series of Oregon Trail Memorial half dollars, and in 2005 special nickels in the Westward Journey series featured the sighting of the Pacific Ocean by Lewis and Clark, at the mouth of the Columbia River.

The "Portland Penny"

A coin like this 1835 Liberty Head cent decided the name of the settlement that would grow into Oregon's largest city. The original coin is now in the Oregon History Center.

1938 Oregon Trail Memorial Half Dollar

This coin honored the pioneers of the Oregon Trail, many of whom lie buried along its 2,000-mile length.

KANSAS

High school students voted for Kansas's final concept, which incorporates both the state animal and the state flower. The bison and the sunflower each played a part in the history of Kansas and were plentiful when it joined the Union. In the 1,600+ ideas submitted, sunflowers appeared more than any other object, including one concept with a banner labeled "There's no place like home" draped across one of the flowers.

34 of 50

Launch festivities were held on September 9, 2005, at the Kansas State Fair. An American bison was on hand when the Wild Women of the Frontier horse-riders group delivered a generous supply of new quarters to the event. Four days later, a trailer en route from the Philadelphia Mint to Birmingham, Alabama, caught on fire, its temperatures exceeding 1,200 degrees. The cargo consisted of $800,000 face value in Kansas quarters, which spilled out on the highway about two miles from the Alabama state line. The coins were examined to see if any could be salvaged, cleaned, and put into circulation.

The Western Meadowlark and the Sunflower, symbols of Kansas

MINTAGE FIGURES

Circulation Coins (copper-nickel)	Proof Coins (copper-nickel)	Proof Coins (silver)
2005-P: 263,400,000 2005-D: 300,000,000	2005-S: 3,262,000	2005-S: 1,606,970

Numismatic**Notes**

Adolph Cohen, a clothier in Leavenworth, was the only Kansas merchant to issue Civil War tokens. Examples today are worth between $900 and $5,000 (in Very Good to Mint State–63 condition). The obverse design is similar to other Civil War tokens, including one struck for Indiana grocers J.L. and G.F. Rowe (pictured). The latter are much more common, and are worth between $15 and $150.

Tokens are shown enlarged.

WEST VIRGINIA

The West Virginia quarter portrays the New River Gorge Bridge, an engineering triumph in the midst of the state's natural splendor. The bridge arches 876 feet above the New River Gorge and spans 3,030 feet. The governor's office received 1,800 design concepts that students at the Governor's School for the Arts reviewed.

35 of 50

The coin's official launch ceremony was held in Charleston on October 14, 2005, on the steps of the State Capitol building. It was the day before Bridge Day, a statewide celebration honoring the span pictured on the quarter. Actors portraying Abraham and Mary Todd Lincoln entertained those present with a dramatic performance.

MINTAGE FIGURES

Circulation Coins (copper-nickel)	Proof Coins (copper-nickel)	Proof Coins (silver)
2005-P: 365,400,000 2005-D: 356,200,000	2005-S: 3,262,000	2005-S: 1,606,970

**The Cardinal and
the Rhododendron,
symbols of West Virginia**

<u>Numismatic</u>Notes

After statehood in June 1863, banks formerly in Virginia found themselves with new West Virginia addresses. This was reflected on changing imprints on currency of banks of the district, similar to the situation in Maine in 1820.

1934–1938 Daniel Boone Bicentennial Half Dollar

In 1776, pioneer Daniel Boone was commissioned as an officer of the Virginia militia when Kentucky formally became a western county of Virginia. After the Revolution, he settled in Kanawha County, in a region of Virginia that would later become part of West Virginia.

1946–1951 Booker T. Washington Memorial Half Dollar

Booker T. Washington was born in Franklin County, Virginia. He was freed from slavery at age 9, at the end of the Civil War, and moved with his family to West Virginia. It was there that he learned to read and write. Washington would grow up to be an influential educator and author, and a spokesman for the nation's recently liberated Black citizens.

Coins are shown enlarged.

NEVADA

Nevada put the Internet to work in its search for the right state quarter concept. After the assigned committee narrowed down the field of received submissions, five designs were posted and votes were accepted from early 2003 until the end of May. The people chose the concept that was eventually minted.

36 of 50

Three galloping wild mustangs are at the center of Nevada's state quarter. Mountains and a rising sun loom in the distance. Sagebrush flanks the horses. This engaging design is called "Morning in Nevada."

The Commission of Fine Arts, in its advisory capacity, had selected another concept as its choice. In the end, the Mint director agreed with the people of Nevada, and Nevada's mustangs galloped their way into numismatic history.

The Mountain Bluebird and the Sagebrush, symbols of Nevada

MINTAGE FIGURES

Circulation Coins (copper-nickel)	Proof Coins (copper-nickel)	Proof Coins (silver)
2006-P: 277,000,000 2006-D: 312,800,000	2006-S: n/a	2006-S: n/a

Numismatic Notes

From 1870 through 1893, the Carson City Mint produced silver and gold coins—mostly Morgan silver dollars and double eagles ($20 gold coins). Since 1942 the structure has housed the Nevada State Museum, which includes a numismatic display. Following the rise of the gambling industry in Nevada, casino chips have become a popular numismatic collectible.

Goldfield, Nevada, in the Early 1900s
This Nevada boomtown was one of many communities that flourished following silver and gold discoveries in the western United States.

**Gold and Silver Coins
from Carson City**

NEBRASKA

Notes from the first meeting of Nebraska's State Quarter Design Committee were posted on the Internet, May 30, 2003. They included this:

37 of 50

> [Jean Gentry, deputy chief counsel from the Treasury] stated there are three elements the Mint will be looking for in a design; these are as follows:

1. Coinability (something that can be reproduced in a large quantity, can be used in vending machines, etc. etc.).

2. Historical accuracy (the Mint will work very closely with the state to make sure every element on the design is historically accurate).

3. Appropriateness (should be dignified and not frivolous).

Nebraska citizens submitted more than 6,500 concepts for their quarter. Farming and homesteading motifs, reflective of the early years of the territory that became a state in 1906, included fields, tractors, crops, and sod huts. The chosen design featured Chimney Rock (a landmark for Forty Niners on the way to California) and a pioneer family in a covered wagon. Governor Dave Heineman made this statement: "I

The Western Meadowlark and the Goldenrod, symbols of Nebraska

chose Chimney Rock because I felt it best represented our state's pioneering spirit and cultural heritage. It reflected the resolve, persistence, and incomparable work ethic that our forbearers brought to the plains."

MINTAGE FIGURES

Circulation Coins (copper-nickel)	Proof Coins (copper-nickel)	Proof Coins (silver)
2006-P: n/a 2006-D: n/a	2006-S: n/a	2006-S: n/a

NUMISMATIC NOTES

The Durham Western History Museum in Omaha houses many coins from the collection of Byron Reed, including an 1804 silver dollar and rare pattern coins. Reed was a Nebraska real estate operator who also collected books and autographs. He worked on his coin collection from the 1880s until his death in 1891. In his will he left his coins and library to the city of Omaha, along with land for a museum.

An 1804 Silver Dollar

Byron Reed owned an example of one of the most famous American coins, the super-rare 1804 Draped Bust silver dollar. When examples are sold at auction, they often bring prices of $1 million or even more.

COLORADO

Two well-known numismatic figures were among the 12-person Colorado Commemorative Quarter Advisory Commission: Chris Cipoletti, executive director of the American Numismatic Association; and Barbara McTurk, former superintendent of the Denver Mint.

38 of 50

Residents of the state were invited to submit written concepts to the governor's office. In the early months of 2004, Frances Owens, first lady of Colorado, began a tour to introduce schoolchildren and others to the state quarter concept, inviting designs to be submitted.

On May 31, 2005, Governor Bill Owens announced his personal choice, which became the adopted design. The central motif featured the Rocky Mountains and the inscription COLORFUL COLORADO. This was the design favored by many Coloradoans and voted as number one by the Citizens Coinage Advisory Committee. The design is scenic, with all of its elements tied together—"the type of motif," says numismatic historian Q. David Bowers, "that, in my opinion, is most pleasing to the eye."

The Lark Bunting and the White and Lavender Columbine, symbols of Colorado

MINTAGE FIGURES

Circulation Coins (copper-nickel)	Proof Coins (copper-nickel)	Proof Coins (silver)
2006-P: n/a 2006-D: n/a	2006-S: n/a	2006-S: n/a

NUMISMATICNOTES

In 1860 and 1861, during the Colorado gold rush, a mint was operated by Clark, Gruber & Co. in Denver. It produced $2.50, $5, $10, and $20 coins. The 1860 versions of the largest two denominations featured a fanciful depiction of Pikes Peak. Also in 1861, J.J. Conway & Co. in Georgia Gulch produced a small number of $2.50, $5, and $10 gold coins, and John Parsons & Co. struck $2.50 and $5 coins near Tarryall. In 1862 the Treasury Department bought the operation of Clark, Gruber & Co. and renamed it the Denver Mint, using that terminology in *Annual Reports*. However, the government did not strike coins there. In 1900 and 1901, in Victor, Colorado, Joseph Lesher issued octagonal medals (called *Lesher referendum dollars*) as a private venture. Most bore advertisements for regional merchants. In 1906 the Denver Mint, in a new building under construction since 1904, opened for business. The American Numismatic Association Headquarters was established in Colorado Springs in 1964.

John Parsons & Co.
$2.50 Gold Piece

J.J. Conway & Co. $5 Gold Piece

Clark, Gruber & Co.
$20 Gold Piece (Reverse)

NORTH DAKOTA

Serious planning for the state's 2006 quarter began on April 14, 2004, when the North Dakota Quarter Design Selection Commission was formed under Governor John Hoeven.

39 of 50

North Dakotans were invited to submit written concepts of up to 50 words before the July 1 deadline. This invitation generated fewer than 400 entries, later sorted into five categories for further evaluation: agriculture; American Indian culture; Badlands; International Peace Gardens; and landscape.

These written concepts were sent to the Mint to be turned into art. In December 2004 the Commission met to review what they received from the Mint, and suggested several revisions. Three were picked as favorites and returned. The favorite of the Commission of Fine Arts featured two grazing bison with a backdrop of the sun rising behind Badlands buttes.

The citizens of North Dakota were asked to choose from the bison design and one depicting geese flying over typical terrain of the state, with a rising sun in the distance.

The Western Meadowlark and the Wild Prairie Rose, symbols of North Dakota

Governor Hoeven made the final choice on June 3, 2005: "Badlands with Bison."

MINTAGE FIGURES

Circulation Coins (copper-nickel)	Proof Coins (copper-nickel)	Proof Coins (silver)
2006-P: n/a 2006-D: n/a	2006-S: n/a	2006-S: n/a

NUMISMATIC NOTES

National Bank Notes from North Dakota are considered by collectors to be especially scarce.

Theodore Roosevelt (pictured) is one of the few great American presidents not represented on coins (except in miniature on the Mount Rushmore commemoratives of 1991 and on the 2006 South Dakota state quarter). He did not make the list of finalists for North Dakota's quarter design. "Rough Rider State," one of North Dakota's nicknames, refers to Roosevelt, who lived there when he was a young man. The inimitable TR is well known to numismatists—as president, he championed a renaissance of American coinage in the early 1900s, encouraging artists such as Augustus Saint-Gaudens and Bela Lyon Pratt to redesign the nation's circulating coins. (Pictured are Pratt's incuse $5 Indian Head design, and Saint-Gaudens's $20 Miss Liberty design.)

SOUTH DAKOTA

A committee set up for the South Dakota quarter considered 50 concepts before settling on five. These were: Mount Rushmore framed by two heads of wheat; Mount Rushmore with a bison in the foreground; Mount Rushmore with a pheasant; a bison framed by wheat; and a pheasant framed by wheat. These were sent to the Mint to be turned into artwork.

40 of 50

To many coin collectors, Mount Rushmore was considered a has-been motif—three different commemoratives honored the famous mountain in 1991, and none were particularly popular at the time.

The Commission of Fine Arts reviewed the motifs and selected a bison standing on a grassy mound, facing right, with its head slightly toward the viewer, with heads of wheat to each side, somewhat reminiscent of the Lincoln wheat cent reverse. *Coin World* writer Paul Gilkes said that the CFA was having a "love fest" with bison. One had recently appeared on a commemorative dollar, another on the 2005 Kansas quarter, and still another on the 2005 nickel.

Nevertheless, when state residents cast nearly 172,000 votes, the winner was a design with Mount Rushmore, a single stalk of wheat to each side, and a Chinese ring-necked pheasant in flight. On April 27, 2005, Governor Mike Rounds confirmed the pick.

The Ring-Necked Pheasant and the Pasque Flower, symbols of South Dakota

MINTAGE FIGURES

Circulation Coins (copper-nickel)	Proof Coins (copper-nickel)	Proof Coins (silver)
2006-P: n/a 2006-D: n/a	2006-S: n/a	2006-S: n/a

NUMISMATIC NOTES

The 1991 Mount Rushmore Golden Anniversary commemorative coins included a half dollar, silver dollar, and $5 gold piece. Of the four presidents depicted—George Washington, Thomas Jefferson, Theodore Roosevelt, and Abraham Lincoln—only Roosevelt has never been the sole occupant of a U.S. coin. He is the only president to have taken an active personal interest in the nation's coinage designs.

1991 Mount Rushmore Commemoratives

The presidents on Mount Rushmore were sculpted by Gutzom Borglum, who earlier had modeled the figures of Stonewall Jackson and Robert E. Lee shown on the Stone Mountain Memorial half dollar (see Georgia).

Some coins are shown enlarged.

MONTANA

Montana residents were invited to submit written concepts for their state quarter, with the deadline set at August 31, 2005. These were reviewed by the Montana Quarter Design Commission, after which residents voted for their favorite.

To Be Issued in 2007

41 of 50

Governor Brian Schweitzer and the Commission selected four designs and sent them to the U.S. Mint in October 2005. One design featured a bull elk at the center with plains extending back to a rock formation and the sun rising in the distance. Another concept had a bison skull in the center with a feather hanging from one horn. Alternatively with this motif, there could be plains in the distance with mountains. Another variation on the same theme had a Native American staff with a feather hanging from it next to the skull. A third concept emphasized the state's nickname, with a mountain range in the distance, a river, and the sky with a few clouds, and the inscription, BIG SKY COUNTRY. The fourth design was an outline of the state enclosing elements including mountains and plains.

The Western Meadowlark and the Bitterroot, symbols of Montana

Numismatic Notes

The United States Assay Office in Helena was a repository for many Morgan silver dollars that upon their release in the 1960s proved to be scarce issues.

Pocket Change of 1889

In 1889, the year Montana became a state, Americans used a mélange of bronze, copper-nickel, silver, and gold coins in day-to-day business. The Indian Head cent had been around since just before the Civil War, and would continue for another 20 years. The nickel three-cent piece was minted for the last time in 1889. The Liberty Head nickel was a relative newcomer, having debuted in 1883; it replaced the Shield nickel that year.

The dime, quarter, and half dollar each featured a scene of Miss Liberty seated with a shield; they would all be replaced by new designs in 1892. The Morgan dollar was the largest silver coin in 1889; and the gold dollar was physically the smallest. Other gold coins of the era included the quarter eagle ($2.50 denomination), the $3 gold piece, the half eagle ($5), the eagle ($10), and the double eagle ($20).

WASHINGTON

The Washington State Quarter Advisory Commission invited written suggestions from the public for the design of their state quarter. The deadline was set as July 30, 2005. By that time, the Commission received 1,150 entries. Governor Christine Gregoire planned to select her favorites by September 30, then submit several written concepts for the U.S. Mint to turn into art.

To Be Issued
in 2007

42 of 50

The five submitted concepts were: a salmon; Mount Rainier and an apple within an outline of Washington state; an apple within the outline of Washington state; an outline of Washington State with Mount Rainier centered; a salmon breaching the water with Mount Rainier as a backdrop; and a Northwest Native American stylized orca. It was suggest that the motto, THE EVERGREEN STATE, be included in at least some of the designs.

It was planned that after the artwork had been returned by the Mint, a public opinion poll would take place. Appropriately guided, the Commission would make its recommendations to the governor in April 2006. A minor scandal erupted during the public polling, when it was revealed that the Web-based ballots had been stuffed—manipulated by automatic computerized voting. State officials were tipped off when more than a million votes were tallied over a single weekend. In response, the online sys-

The Willow Goldfinch and
the Coast Rhododendron,
symbols of Washington

tem was revamped for another vote. On may 4, Governor Chris Gregoire announced and confirmed the people's choice: a salmon leaping in front of Mount Ranier.

Numismatic Notes

In 1925, commemorative half dollars were struck to honor the centennial of Fort Vancouver.

1925 Fort Vancouver Centennial Half Dollar

This coin features a portrait of John McLoughlin, who built Fort Vancouver on the Columbia River in 1825. The half dollars were struck to be sold at $1 apiece, to raise money for the fort's 100-year celebrations. Although they were struck in San Francisco, they do not bear the S mintmark. The coin's models were prepared by Laura Gardin Fraser, a talented artist whose husband had created the Buffalo nickel design.

Coin is shown enlarged.

IDAHO

Governor Dirk Kempthorne tapped the Idaho Commission of the Arts to oversee the state's design submission process and to review ideas. Citizens of Idaho were invited to submit written concepts of up to 150 words until September 9, 2005. To encourage more participation, residents were also invited to submit art, but the governor hastened to say

43 of 50

that the U.S. Mint would create its sketches only from written ideas. Multiple submissions from the same person were allowed.

Further, "Simplicity should be emphasized; designs that include too many elements become cluttered and are discouraged."

By the September deadline, more than 1,200 ideas had been received. The Commission sorted through them and selected 10 to be presented to Governor Kempthorne, who then narrowed the field down to five. These were a peregrine falcon with the state motto ESTO PERPETUA; the Sawtooth Mountains; farmland tapestry showing an aerial view of cropland; two lines from the state song "Here We Have Idaho" flanking an outline of the state; and "bold and distinctive," the latter having the word IDAHO prominently across the center of the coin.

The Mountain Bluebird and the Syringa, symbols of Idaho

NumismaticNOTES

In 1890, the year Idaho became a state, Congress passed the Sherman Silver Purchase Act, sponsored by Senator John Sherman of Ohio. This was President Benjamin Harrison's concession to the silver mining interests in the Western states, in return for their support of the McKinley Tariff Act (which attempted to protect American industry by setting the average tariff at an incredible 48%—the highest peacetime rate ever). Under the Sherman Act, the U.S. Treasury was required to buy, at market price, 4.5 million ounces of silver every month—almost the entire production of the nation's mines. The silver was purchased with federal Treasury Notes redeemable in gold or silver; most of these notes were immediately redeemed for gold, which was then sent overseas, drastically draining the nation's reserves. The Sherman Silver Purchase Act was a failure, and it was repealed in 1893.

Series of 1890 $2 Treasury Note

Treasury Notes (also known as *Coin Notes*), such as this $2 example, were used to pay for silver purchased under the Sherman Act. These notes are popular and widely collected today; the $2 Treasury Note, Series of 1890, was voted number 15 among the *100 Greatest American Currency Notes* (Bowers/Sundman, 2006). (The number 1 spot went to the $1,000 bill of the same series, called the *Grand Watermelon Note*.)

Note is shown reduced.

WYOMING

Governor David D. Freudenthal set up the Wyoming Coinage Advisory Committee and named stamp collector Jack Rosenthal chairman. Rosenthal had chaired the U.S. Postal Service's Citizens' Stamp Advisory Committee in Washington, DC.

To Be Issued in 2007

44 of 50

The committee's first meeting was in Cheyenne on January 13, 2005. The goal was to collect and finalize designs by September, at which time no more than five were to be submitted to the Mint, where art would be created.

Residents were allowed to submit words only, up to 50 of them, by completing the statement, "I think the back of the Wyoming quarter should show...." The deadline was April 30. More than 1,300 people filled out the form. The Committee selected five designs, four of which depicted a bucking horse with rider, with various differences in the background and details. The fifth concept was Old Faithful, the famous geyser in Yellowstone National Park, as taken from a stamp issued in 1934.

The Western Meadowlark and the Indian Paintbrush, symbols of Wyoming

NUMISMATICNOTES

In 1999 the Mint struck commemorative silver dollars honoring Yellowstone National Park. About 24,000 were sold in Uncirculated finish, and nearly 130,000 in Proof—somewhat low quantities for a modern commemorative coin. As with all U.S. commemoratives, both versions (Uncirculated and Proof) share the same design. On this silver dollar, a geyser is shown in full blast, with Yellowstone's park landscape surrounding. (The park has more geysers, hot springs, steam vents, and mud spots than exist in the rest of the world combined.) On the reverse, an American bison—the largest animal in the park's ecosystem—dominates the motif, with mountains and the rising sun in the background. Yellowstone is the nation's first (and the world's oldest) national park; it was dedicated by an act of Congress, signed by President Ulysses Grant, on March 1, 1872. Half the proceeds from the sale of this coin went to support Yellowstone, with the other half assigned to other national parks.

1999 Yellowstone National Park Silver Dollar

UTAH

On September 17, 2004, Utah Governor Olene Walker created the Utah Quarter Dollar Commemorative Coin Commission. He appointed as chairman H. Robert Campbell, a Salt Lake City numismatist and past president of the American Numismatic Association. The Commission had three other members: Frank McEntire, director of the Utah Arts Council;

To Be Issued in 2007

45 of 50

Patti Harrington, superintendent of public instruction of the Utah State Office of Education; and Phil Notarianni, director of the Utah State Historical Society.

The public was invited to send concepts until March 1, 2005, after which the Commission would select five favorites to be submitted to the governor, who would select up to all five to send on to the U.S. Mint.

The Commission presented its five choices to Governor Jon Huntsman on July 29, 2005. Huntsman picked out three and sent them to the Mint. One motif illustrated the 1869 transcontinental railroad ceremony at Promontory Point. Another showed a beehive, symbol of industry and long an icon associated with the district, including on the Mormon $5 gold coin of 1860. The third illustrated winter sports, reflecting the state's prominence in that field and its 2002 hosting of the Winter Olympics.

The American Seagull and the Sego Lily, symbols of Utah

Online voting began in the second quarter of 2006; as of press time, the winner has not been selected.

NUMISMATIC NOTES

In 1849 and 1850, Mormon gold pieces were struck under the supervision of Brigham Young, in a little adobe mint building in Salt Lake City. In 1860, a $5 gold piece was struck. The 2002 Salt Lake Olympic Games were commemorated by silver dollars and $5 gold coins.

Brigham Young

1849 Mormon $20 Gold Piece

This was the first coin of the $20 denomination struck in the United States (Utah had been purchased by the U.S. after the Mexican War). The federal government would make its first circulating $20 coins, called *double eagles*, in 1850.

1860 Mormon $5 Gold Piece

An early name for the Utah territory was the *State of Deseret*, the last word meaning "honeybee." Joseph Smith and Brigham Young used the beehive (seen on the reverse of this coin) as a Mormon symbol.

OKLAHOMA

Information about the Oklahoma quarter's design-selection process was not available at press time. However, the following facts about the state of Oklahoma may give clues as to what the design will turn out to be: *Statehood*— November 16, 1907. *Capital*— Oklahoma City. *Nickname*— Sooner State. *Land area and rank*—68,679 square miles (19th

To Be Issued in 2008

46 of 50

largest state). *Largest city*—Oklahoma City. *State motto*—Labor Omnia Vincit (Labor conquers all things). *State flower*—Mistletoe. *State bird*—Scissor-tailed flycatcher. *State tree*—Redbud. *State animal*—Bison. *State song*—"Oklahoma."

Theodore Roosevelt Inaugural Medal

Roosevelt was president when Oklahoma became a state in 1907.

The Scissor-Tailed Flycatcher and the Mistletoe, symbols of Oklahoma

NUMISMATIC NOTES

National Bank Notes from the Territory of Oklahoma, before statehood, are especially highly prized by collectors.

In 1907, the year Oklahoma became a state, a coin was born that many people consider the most beautiful in United States history. The Saint-Gaudens $20 gold piece had about 12,000 coins struck for circulation. These were made with a high relief, which proved inconvenient for production and for stacking. Later in the year more than 360,000 coins were struck with a lower relief. The coins would be made into the early 1930s.

Before the circulation-strike coins were issued, a pattern with an even higher relief had been made. These Ultra High Relief coins are very rare, and worth $2 million or more.

1907 Ultra High Relief $20 Pattern

Coin is shown enlarged.

NEW MEXICO

Information about the design-selection process for the New Mexico quarter was not available at press time. However, the following facts about the state of New Mexico may give clues as to what the design will turn out to be: *Statehood*—January 6, 1912. *Capital*—Santa Fe. *Nickname*—Land of Enchantment. *Land area and rank*—121,365 square miles

To Be Issued in 2008

47 of 50

(5th largest state). *Largest city*—Albuquerque. *State motto*—Crescit Euodo (It grows at it goes). *State flower*—Yucca. *State bird*—Roadrunner. *State tree*—Piñon. *State song*—"O, Fair New Mexico; Asi Es Nuevo Mexico."

Presidents Taft and Wilson

When New Mexico became a state in January 1912, William Howard Taft was president—the first president of the contiguous 48 states, after Arizona joined the Union in February. Both of the new states, however, went to his Democratic opponent, Woodrow Wilson, who won the White House that November.

The Roadrunner and the Yucca Flower, symbols of New Mexico

NUMISMATIC NOTES

Paper money collectors avidly seek National Bank Notes from the Territory of New Mexico, printed before it became a state. In fact, all such paper money of the territories is uncommon and desirable.

National Bank Notes began with the National Banking Act of 1863, a piece of legislation passed to help raise money to fight the Civil War. If a state-chartered bank were judged to have a good reputation, it would be allowed to apply to become a National Bank. From 1863 to 1935, more than 10,000 National Banks issued notes with their own imprints and designs, in various denominations.

**Territory of New Mexico
National Bank Note**

This Series of 1882 Brown Back $10 note is from the First National Bank of Santa Rosa.

Note is shown reduced.

ARIZONA

In November 2005, Governor Janet Napolitano of Arizona established a commission to recommend designs for the new state quarter. On December 13 she announced that 22 members had been chosen. The panel was composed of representatives from the state legislature, historical and art societies, schoolteachers, and members of the general public. By

To Be Issued in 2008

48 of 50

that time the semi-annual Grand Canyon State Poll, conducted by telephone by Northern Arizona University Social Research Laboratory in Flagstaff, had included the subject in a recent survey. Most respondents preferred a scene from nature, such as the Grand Canyon or a saguaro cactus, instead of state emblems or representations of history.

The commission was charged with selecting up to five concepts to be submitted to the U.S. Mint in September 2006. Perhaps the following facts about the state of Arizona give clues as to what the design will turn out to be: *Statehood*—February 14, 1912. *Capital*—Phoenix. *Nickname*—Grand Canyon State. *Land area and rank*—111,642 square miles (6th largest state). *Largest city*—Phoenix. *State motto*—Ditat Deus (God enriches). *State flower*—Blossom of the saguaro cactus. *State bird*—Cactus wren. *State tree*—Paloverde. *State animal*—Ringtail cat. *State song*—"Arizona March Song."

The Cactus Wren and the Saguaro Cactus Blossom, symbols of Arizona

NUMISMATIC NOTES

National Bank Notes from the Territory of Arizona, printed before the territory became a state, are especially highly prized by today's collectors.

Pocket Change of 1912

In 1912, the year Arizona became a state, a variety of bronze, copper-nickel, silver, and gold coins were in circulation. The Lincoln cent was a relative newcomer, having debuted in 1909. The Liberty Head nickel, part of America's pocket change since 1883, was nearing the end of its run; it would be replaced by the Buffalo nickel in 1913. The Barber dime, quarter, and half dollar—all introduced in 1892—were also

close to extinction. In 1916 they would be replaced by three new classics: the Mercury dime, the Standing Liberty quarter, and the Liberty Walking half dollar. Silver dollars hadn't been minted since 1904. Gold coins struck in 1912 include the quarter eagle ($2.50 denomination), the half eagle ($5), the eagle ($10), and the double eagle ($20).

ALASKA

The Alaska Commemorative Coin Commission, established in 2005, had 11 members. The agendas of its meetings, held in Anchorage the first Thursday of each month, were posted on the Internet, as were the minutes. Residents of the state were invited to submit design concepts from January 1 to February 28, 2006. Perhaps the following facts about the state of Alaska

To Be Issued
in 2008

49 of 50

give clues as to what the design will turn out to be: *Statehood*—January 3, 1959. *Capital*—Juneau. *Nickname*—The Last Frontier (unofficial). *Land area and rank*—570,374 square miles (largest state). *Largest city*—Anchorage. *State motto*—North to the future. *State flower*—Forget-me-not. *State bird*—Willow ptarmigan. *State tree*—Sitka spruce. *State animal*—Moose. *State song*—"Alaska's Flag."

1990 Eisenhower Centennial Dollar
Dwight D. Eisenhower was president when Alaska became a state in late February 1959.

**The Willow Ptarmigan
and the Forget-Me-Not,
symbols of Alaska**

NUMISMATIC NOTES

Tokens of the Alaska Rural Rehabilitation Corporation were issued in 1935. Today they are listed in the *Guide Book of United States Coins*.

These tokens, intended for the colonists of the Matanuska Valley Colonization Project, were called *Bingles* (possibly after a prominent preacher of the valley). They were issued by the federal government according to the number of dependents in a family. They were redeemable only in ARRC stores, and only saw about six months of circulation, in 1935 and early 1936. After that the tokens were redeemed for regular U.S. coins and destroyed.

1935 Alaska Rural Rehabilitation Corporation Tokens

Denominations ranged from one cent to one dollar in aluminum, and five and ten dollars in brass.

HAWAII

Information on the design-selection process for the Hawaii quarter was not available at press time. However, the following facts about the state of Hawaii may give clues as to what the design will turn out to be: *Statehood*—August 21, 1959. *Capital*—Honolulu. *Nickname*—Aloha State. *Land area and rank*—6,423 square miles (47th largest state). *Largest city*—Honolulu. *State motto*—The life of the land is perpetuated in righteousness. *State flower*—Yellow hibiscus. *State bird*—Hawaiian goose. *State tree*—Kukui (candlenut). *State marine animal*—Humpback whale. *State song*—"Hawai'i Pono'i."

To Be Issued
in 2008

50 of 50

Eisenhower Dollar

A new dollar coin—the first struck since 1935—was introduced into circulation in 1971. It featured a portrait of Dwight Eisenhower, who was president when Hawaii became a state in 1959.

**The Nene and
the Pua Aloalo,
symbols of Hawaii**

NUMISMATIC NOTES

In 1847 King Kamehameha of Hawaii issued copper cents (struck in Massachusetts). In 1883, silver dimes, quarter dollars, half dollars, and dollars, with a total face value $1 million, were struck in San Francisco (but with no mintmark) for the kingdom. National Bank Notes with territorial addresses, including those of pre-statehood Hawaii, are especially popular with today's paper money collectors. In the 1940s, $1, $5, $10, and $20 bills were issued during World War II overprinted with the word HAWAII, to make them easily cancelable if the Japanese took over the islands.

1928 Hawaiian Sesquicentennial Half Dollar

Fewer than 10,000 of these commemorative half dollars (and 50 special Proof presentation pieces) were struck to honor the 150th anniversary of the arrival of Captain James Cook to the Hawaiian Islands in 1778. At the time that these were issued, they sold for the highest initial sale price of any U.S. commemorative coin: $2 apiece. Today an Uncirculated example is worth between $2,500 and $6,000 or more.

Coin is shown enlarged.

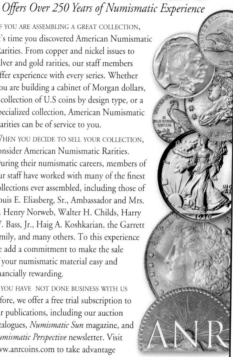

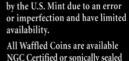

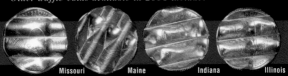